I0023278

VOLUME

3

REAL ESTATE INVESTING

Tax Lien and Tax Deed Sales

Copyright © 2011 Hennin
All rights reserved.
ISBN-13: 978-1-933039-63-3

Library of Congress -in-Publication Data

All rights reserved. No part of this book or applicable additions may be reproduced in any form or by any means.
Printed in the United States of America

10 9 8 7 6 5 4 3 2 1

The enclosed material is designed for educational purposes only. Each State may have different certification and specific guidelines. Please refer to your State for additional and future information. The information contained herein is considered correct at the time of creation but laws and regulations are updated frequently and the reader assumes the responsibility for confirming current regulations and applicable data. The publisher and author make no warranty as to the success of the individuals using the training material contained herein. The publisher and author make no warranty as to any action taken by any individual completing this program. The reader is responsible for the appropriate use of the materials and information provided. This publication is designed to provide accurate and authoritative information concerning the subject matter. All material is sold with the understanding that neither the author nor the publisher guarantees the actions of any individual making use of the inclusions. Neither the author nor the publisher is rendering a legal opinion, accounting recommendation or other professional service. If legal advice or other expert assistance is desired, the services of a legal professional or other individual should be sought. The applicable federally released forms, disclosures and notices are generated from public domain. Copyright law does apply to all intellectual materials and all rights under said law are reserved b y the copyright owner.

Coursework is available at special quantity discounts to use as premiums and sales promotions within corporate or private training programs. To obtain information or inquire about availability please write to Director, PO Box 1, Hollidaysburg, PA 16648.

NOTICE

The enclosed materials are copyrighted materials. Federal law prohibits the unauthorized reproduction, distribution or exhibit of the materials. The materials contained within this publication are distributed for personal use.
Violations of copyright law will be prosecuted.

From the US Code Collection – Violation of Copyright is a Criminal Offense

Criminal Infringement—Any person who infringes a copyright willfully either

> (1)   for the purpose of commercial advantage or private financial gain or

> (2)   by the reproduction or distribution, including by electronic means during any 180-day
>   period, of 1 or more copyrighted works, shall be punished as provided under section 2319 of title 18,
> United States Code.

In General.—except as otherwise provided by this title, an infringer of copyright is liable for

> (1)   the copyright owner's actual damages and any additional profits of the
>   Infringer

> (2)   statutory damages

Violations of copyright will be prosecuted as allowed under law.

Copyright © 2011 Hennin
All rights reserved.
ISBN-13: 978-1-933039-63-3

REAL ESTATE INVESTING
Tax Lien and Tax Deed Sales

Tax Sale Profits Do Happen

Tax Sale investment offers an incredible opportunity to obtain real estate for pennies on the dollar. The savvy investor who gains an understanding of the essential research requirements of the successful tax sale investor, creates a solid foundation of knowledge of the tax sale opportunities that exists and generates an investment strategy that enables diversification and secure streams of income will have the tools necessary to challenge wealth and succeed with tax sale-investment opportunities .

C ongratulations on your decision to enter the exciting and lucrative field of tax sale investment. Over the coming weeks you will gain the knowledge and tools, you need to capitalize on the unlimited opportunities available to you through investment at tax sales and deeds. Real estate investment has enabled more Americans to achieve millionare status than nearly any other opportunity available today. Now, you too can challenge wealth and succeed with tax sale-investment opportunities.

The design of this coursework will provide you with the building blocks you will use to create the solid foundation necessary to begin building your real estate empire. You will obtain the knowledge you will require to implement the techniques and strategies necessary to make your tax sale investment experience successful.

You have purchased one of the most powerful and comprehensive tax sale-investment courses available on the market. The tools and knowledge incorporated throughout the program will enable you to use the opportunity available within the arena of tax sale investments as the primary tool to grow you investment portfolio, obtain an exceptional return on each investment dollar you place and reach for the American Dream of millionaire status!

Upon completion of the coursework, you will be able to attend and bid at tax sale with confidence and security that you have the solid foundation of knowledge and tools that will enable you to achieve the success you deserve.

- You will identify the three most common tax-sale investment opportunities that may play a part in your ultimate strategy and goals.

- You will gain a comprehensive understanding of the investment ramifications of each sale so you can isolate how each investment opportunity can enhance your investment strategy.

- You will obtain knowledge of the fundamentals of real estate that will enable you to research each potential investment. This will enable you to conduct the applicable research and ensure that you stabilize your investment portfolio to minimize risk.

- You will gain an understanding of the right of taxation and the ramifications of this right, including the creation of the opportunity to make the investment in tax sale liens or deeds. You will learn how to use this right to assist you in generating potential cash savings strategies after you have made your first investment.

- You will obtain the tools necessary to generate a solid investment strategy that includes completing realistic long and short-term investment strategy goals.

- You will learn to assess how you might employ each type of sale to enable you to generate a well-rounded portfolio that secures your investment dollars and minimizes risk.

Each chapter within this coursework is critical to your success in the exciting and lucrative arena of tax sale investments. It is vital that you view the coursework as a set of building blocks and complete each level of training before moving onto the next level. This building of your skill base will help you to create the solid foundation upon which you will build your real estate empire.

This program is created for the investor who desires full rights to the property investment.

This course is essential for the investor who requires an incredible return on their investment dollars unsurpassed in other investment offerings.

This manual is essential for the individual looking to secure the future of themselves and their family through the attainment of the American Dream of homeownership.

No matter what your ultimate goal is for the use of the tax sale investment tools you will gain, this program contains the information you need to develop a framework that will assist you in forming a workable plan and implementing these strategies to reach for your dreams.

Tax sale investments provide several exciting opportunities. You can choose to take advantage of one, some, or all of these potentially life-changing investments available every day around the country. Regardless of the path you take, purchasing this course is the first and most critical step on your pathway to success.

An Investor will learn the strategies, pitfalls and sales parameters that will enable them to build a real estate portfolio of residential and commercial rentals quickly and with less money out of pocket than with nearly any other opportunity. The perceptive investor will utilize the tools and knowledge incorporated throughout this course to generate a well-rounded strategy that minimizes risk and ensures investment success.

Tax sale opportunities increase your ability to attain investment success with lower out of pocket expenses and, through careful scrutiny of each title, lower risk.

Real estate investors will learn how to use tax deed sales to gain access to easily restored and quickly sold flip properties.

Deed investments enable you to invest a small amount of money, flip the property for a huge return and invest those returns in still more real estate.

The first and most essential rule of successful real estate investment is to gain as much leverage as possible using other people's money. By purchasing and restoring your first property for flipping it on the general market for ready cash, you can use the funds provided by your purchaser to buy still more property.

These future purchases can then be flipped or rented to assist you in building your portfolio faster than any other investment strategy you will encounter.

A comprehensive understanding of each type of tax sale you might encounter will enable you to build an investment strategy that helps you to minimize your risk through a diversification of investments. You will learn the elements necessary to allow you to invest in a mixture of the different of types of tax sale opportunities.

- You can gain free and clear deeds for property with no liability.

- You may place some investment funds in tax lien certificates for a stabilized return on your investment dollar.

- You will be able to purchase subject to property for the potentially huge immediate return at a sheriff's sale.

By diversifying your investment portfolio, you will be following the strategy of the professional investor by using all types of opportunities, minimizing your risk exposure and ensuring a steady flow of cash while simultaneously building your overall net worth. This ability to diversify your portfolio quickly and easily creates a higher probability for long-term success than nearly any other real estate strategy.

An individual can obtain the American Dream of homeownership with less money and fewer guidelines than with any conventional method of purchase. Through prudent planning and research, an individual can use the opportunity that exists within the tax-sale investment arena to usurp the requirements of traditional mortgage finance and minimize the cost of homeownership to your family. Owning a home of your own has long been held out as the standard of the American Dream but many individuals do not reach this height. Now, through tax sale opportunity, you can achieve this pinnacle.

Have you ever been told that your dream of homeownership must wait because you just do not qualify today?

- Your credit score is too low

- You have not worked at this job long enough

- You have too much debt

- You need more money down

When you attend a tax sale and purchase a property using the tools incorporated into this program, these issues do not matter. Whether one, some or all of the most common mortgage denial reasons apply to you, tax sale purchases now give you the ability to buy the home of your dreams!

By completing this coursework, you will gain the comprehensive knowledge of tax sale opportunities that will enable you to achieve the dream of homeownership.

- You will learn to buy the home you need without the lending guidelines that have been holding you back.

- You will learn to buy the home you dream about for only a fraction of its real value.

- You will be able to gain access to the tax sale lists, properly research the chain of title, walk into the sale with confidence and grab that dream!

A tax-lien certificate investor can obtain a stable rate of return that exceeds other offerings with their investment dollars. The return that can be achieved through tax lien certificate-investment surpasses what can be gained through nearly any other investment.

Tax lien certificates enable the investor who does not wish to build a real estate empire to profit from tax sale opportunities. This type of investor often desires a higher return on their investment dollars than other opportunities provide. These investors often forget that there are methods they may employ to gain an interest in the stable investment of real estate without the responsibility of holding the actual property.

This course will assist the investor in placing their hard-earned dollars in a high return, low risk venture that is virtually unsurpassed by other investment opportunities.

You will learn to acquire a secure lien against real property that returns 18%, 25% even 50% on the dollar.

A secured lien dictates that if the expected return is not provided within a specified time you get the property to liquidate at sheriff sale.

Gaining the property on any lien not fully paid has the potential to provide you with a return hundreds, even thousands of times in excess of your expectations.

Real estate investment opportunities have enabled more Americans to reach millionaire status than nearly any other medium available today. Through tax sale investments, you can join the millionaires of America faster, investing only pennies on the dollar for each property and gaining access to a tool that you can use throughout your real estate career. Begin today with what you have, invest prudently and climb the millionaire mile!

Regardless of your tax-sale investment goals and dreams, this course will provide you with a fundamental education in tax sale opportunity unavailable from traditional education and previously only provided through apprenticeship to a successful investor or through the trial and error method. This course is designed to provide you with all of the basic knowledge and advanced strategies you will need to walk into the sale confident and secure that you can make the right decision. You will have gained all of the information necessary to confidently research each property and avoid the pitfalls that can exist for the unschooled who enter the tax-sale investment arena. You will obtain the solid foundation to ensure you earn the highest return possible through the strategy that works best for you.

Tax sale profits DO happen. Tax Sale investment offers an incredible opportunity to obtain real estate for pennies on the dollar. Congratulations, on your decision to become a well-informed investor who gains an understanding of the essential research requirements of the successful tax sale investor, create a solid foundation of knowledge of the tax sale opportunities that exist, generate an investment strategy that enables diversification, and secure streams of income. You will have the tools necessary to challenge wealth and win.

CHAPTER

1

TYPES OF SALES

Three common tax sales are available across the country to enable you to meet your investment needs, generate a well-rounded strategy and gain the highest potential return for every investment dollar you place. Each sale carries different benefits, challenges, ramifications and opportunities for the real estate investor. The investment strategy you create may use one, two or all three types of sales. It is important that you gain a comprehensive understanding of each type of sale available to you within the tax sale arena. Each sale can affect the offerings of the other types of sales and a sale you have not considered as an opportunity may be the sale that enables you to round out your investment strategy and reach your goals.

Ministerial	-	Upset Sale	-	Subject To
Judicial	-	Foreclosure Sale	-	Free and Clear
Certificate	-	Tax Lien Certificate		

I f a property owner does not pay the levied taxes as required; the property will eventually be taken in an effort to collect the monies owed for taxes against that property. The taking of the property is an attempt by the taxing authority to meet the budget needs as planned.

- Some States will complete a judicial foreclosure process that enables the State to nullify the delinquent taxpayer's interest in the title in the property. The State is then able to transfer the title to the property to a real estate investor during the tax sale process. This foreclosure action leads to what is commonly termed the Free and Clear sale or the judicial tax sale.

- At other times, a State or Jurisdiction will offer a property that has not completed the foreclosure processes required for a Judicial Sale but at which the delinquent taxpayer's interest is abolished. During this sale, the deed to the property is offered subject to all existing matters of record recorded for public review. This type of sale places the investor gaining the deed to the property in the same position that the delinquent taxpayer held. This sale process is often termed the Subject To or Upset Sale.

- Some States have the authority to create a lien for taxes owed against the piece of property and offer this lien for sale to investors who have cash available to provide the taxing authority. This cash enables the taxing authority to meet the planned budget needs for the fiscal year. The investor obtains interest penalty returns on the money owed when the delinquent taxpayer redeems the certificate. The tax lien takes precedence over all other liens except federal and previously recorded tax liens held against the property regardless of the priority of time. The process of creating a lien investment leads to what is known Tax Lien Certificate Sale.

Following the tax sale, the property owner may or may not have a certain period known as a redemption period during which they can reclaim or clear the title to the property. This redemption period enables the delinquent taxpayer to pay the monies owed plus interest and penalties and reverse the transfers provided during the tax sale process.

- A certificate investor will strive for sales that provide the best redemption terms on the certificates created, as this is how they will make a profit.

- A deed investor will typically gain a profit when the delinquent taxpayer redeems the property during the redemption period, however the deed investor will lose any claim to the property if the delinquent owner redeems the lien.

Specific redemption periods and abilities vary by State or Jurisdiction and it is important that you gain an understanding of the redemption allowances within the investment arenas you choose so that you will be prepared for all potential post-sale alterations that could affect your strategy.

To reclaim the title during the redemption period, the property owner, or any lien holder with an interest in the property, may make full payment for the taxes owed against the property, any penalties imposed and any interest accumulated against the back taxes. Paying these funds in full to the taxing authority causes the lien against the property to be removed and the title is returned to its original status. The investor at who placed their funds at the applicable sale will receive a return of the money invested plus the interest allowed under Statute or the accepted interest bid at the sale.

If payment is not remitted during the redemption period, the tax deed will become the property of the tax deed investor and the tax lien certificate may be converted to a tax deed enabling the certificate investor to gain full access to the property.

DEED SALES

The highest bidder for a property at a tax deed sale receives the deed interest held by the taxing authority. Regardless of the sale type, the original owner's interest in the property is abolished due to the right of taxation. This sale typically follows an auction style process where the taxing authority sets the minimum acceptable bid and the interested investors bid against each other until one is the clear winner.

Upon entering the sale, all bidders will register with the individuals assigned to monitor the sale. Registration may sometimes be limited by a variety of factors.

Example: It is common practice in some States to require that individuals may only bid if they are not currently in arrears on any real estate tax payment to any taxing authority. If this ruling exists at a sale that you attend, you will be asked to sign a statement confirming your status concerning delinquent taxes.

Example: Some States have implemented residency requirements that state that only individuals who are United States citizens or who live within a specific jurisdiction may invest at the sale. If such a ruling exists at a sale that you attend, you will be required to provide proof of your residency status.

Example: Many States require that any individual who plans to invest at tax sale provide proof of their identity and true address prior to placing any bid. If such a requirement exists, you will be asked to show valid identification detailing your name and physical residence during the registration process.

The registration requirements of most sales are not onerous or difficult to meet, however it is important that you understand the requirements set forth for any sale you attend. The ability to bid will be set by Statute or Jurisdictional Decree and you must meet these requirements in order to profit from tax sales. You can obtain the bidding registration rules from the county courthouse of the region that you choose for your investment forays before the date of the sale.

The processes that occur both before and at tax deed sales are specifically outlined for each area. These dictates often require the taxing authority to make detailed preparations before the sale. All practices as set forth by Statute and designated by Jurisdiction must be carefully followed. The compliance with these guidelines will be the duty of the individuals empowered to conduct the sale. It is enough for your investment strategy that you understand that lengthy and detailed processes have been followed to bring the property to the sale.

Many of the guidelines are in place to ensure that the owner whose interest is being abolished by the tax sale obtains adequate warning regarding the taxing authority's intent to sell the deed. The notice to the property owner assists in removing any potential objection that the owner may make in the future. If the owner does not receive the proper notices of the intent of the taxing authority to sell the deed to the property, the owner may obtain a reversal of the sale at a court proceeding.

The owner will receive notices that outline the actions that must be taken for the owner to retain their rights in the property. By the time you attend the sale, the owner of record has essentially released his interest in the property through failure to comply with the options outlined in the warnings provided to them from the taxing authority, courts, and other parties.

TYPICAL DEED SALE PROCESS

- A property owner will fail to pay tax assessment billings for a specified period causing the taxing authority to send notices as required within the Jurisdiction to the property owner indicating that the property will be sold at a tax deed sale.

- Upon the expiration of the allowed term of redemption, or period of payment opportunity, set forth in the notices provided to the property owner, the court will issue a tax deed title or instigate a foreclosure upon the property. Again, the owner of record will receive ample notice that these processes are occurring.

   This foreclosure allows the court to sell the actual ownership interest in the property, either in full or partial ownership interest, to the successful bidder at the planned sale.

   It is important to understand that in the tax deed sale, the property owner typically loses their interest in the property.

There are two common types of deed sale offerings available to the real estate investor. The specific terminology used to define these sales will vary by region, but the most common terms used to define the deed sale offerings are the free and clear and the subject to tax deed sale. Regardless of the terminology, the essence of the two types of sales will remain the same. Each sale provides very specific opportunities and rights to the successful investor and it is critical that you gain an understanding of the interest you will gain at each sale and the ramifications of the sale types.

Free and Clear or Judicial Sale

One type of sale that you might consider when generating your investment plan is the free and clear sale or judicial deed sale. The property sold at this type of sale has undergone a judicial foreclosure process. This process frees the title of all liens and other encumbrances except those placed by federal, state and jurisdictional taxing authorities.

- The taxing authority typically completes, or uses an outside agency to complete, a search on the title to ascertain what, if any other liens may fall against the property.

- The taxing authority then uses the government rights of priority to remove the other liens that may be held against that property. This is completed through a specific notice to the lien holders of the intended action followed by a foreclosure proceeding.

- The taxing authority will complete a full foreclosure process to gain control of the property and to remove any interest held by any lien holder or other interested party.

  NOTE: It is vital that the investor be aware that the taxing authority will typically not remove any liens placed by the IRS or State Taxing Authority. In most instances, the county and school tax assessments will be incorporated into the minimum bid amount you must place at the auction.

  NOTE: An important factor to consider is that there is often a delay period between the date of the foreclosure and the date the tax sale actually occurs.

              During this delay period, additional liens or other matters may be recorded or actions taken against the property.

It is essential that you research the title to any tax sale purchase before placing a bid. This research will enable you to ascertain what, if any, obligations you may be taking on when you purchase the tax sale deed. We have incorporated the essential components of title research later in this coursework. If you desire a more detailed understanding of the title search process, you may want to consider completing a course that is aimed toward providing comprehensive career training in title abstracting.

- It is critical that you locate and understand any matter that affects the title to any property or the rights inherent in any real estate purchase you are considering as an investment.

- Conducting appropriate research as we have outlined in this manual will enable you to feel confident that you comprehend the rights inherent in your investment and secure the funds you are placing.

The free and clear tax sale typically occurs only after the courts have attempted to sell the property using a subject to tax sale process. The bargains available through investment at a free and clear deed sale are obvious.

- The investor is gaining full interest in the property being offered at the tax sale subject only to those specific liens held by federal and state taxing authority and any other matter that is recorded following the judicial foreclosure.

Upon completion of this program, you will have gained a better understanding of how to investigate the title to each potential investment within the public records system. This ability is one skill that many investors at the sale will not have obtained.

- You can walk into the sale confident that you have a complete understanding of the position of each property.

- You can bid on each property offered for sale secure in the knowledge that you understand what potential obligations and rights you are gaining.

- You will turn small investment dollars into huge real estate holdings!

Subject To or Ministerial Sale

A second type of deed sale you may encounter during your tax sale-investment career is the Subject To Sale also termed the Ministerial Sale.

- A subject to process would allow any existing liens or other matters to remain against the property.

This type of sale often frightens new and experienced tax sale investors because many do not fully understand the research that will enable them to gain a comprehensive view of the position of the title being offered at the tax sale. The potential for you at this type of sale is immense. Through a comprehensive understanding of the ramification of these sales and the knowledge of the public records system that will enable you to conduct adequate research, you will gain the investment advantage that enables you to know which property is an exceptional bargain at these sales.

The processes leading to the subject to sale are less complex and time-consuming for the taxing authority as they simply upset the position of the delinquent taxpayer and do not complete the judicial foreclosure actions. This creates the need for you, as the investor, to conduct additional research into the title of the property than you must when completing preparations for the free and clear sale. However, the potential for incredible returns on your investments is increased proportionally.

Often times, investors are surprised to discover that the subject to sale can offer even more opportunity than the free and clear sale.

- The drawback is that you must gain a comprehensive understanding of the research requirements that will enable you to locate these potential bargains.

- The benefit to completing this course is that you are gaining the knowledge base necessary to complete this research!

Many of the investors attending the tax sales in your region will not have the comprehensive knowledge base of research processes that you are gaining and thus you will be one of the most knowledgeable individuals in the auction room.

> The subject to tax sale provides protections for the interest of other parties who have a monetary lien against the property. This protection is in place because the taxing authority has not completed a full judicial foreclosure process but simply revoked the rights and interests of the delinquent taxpayer using the rights of the government to impose taxes on each property and rights set by statute to seize real property if the taxpayer fails to pay the taxes imposed.

> Because the investor is purchasing the property at the ministerial sale subject to other liens, encumbrances and other defects of the title, the need for the investor to complete a detailed search into the property title becomes even greater. This search will enable the investor determine what, if any, liens, judgments, encumbrances, and title defects may exist in regards to the property.

In preparation for the subject to sale, the taxing authority abolishes the rights of the original owner. This process of upsetting the owner's interest is completed through the courts. The taxing authority is able to take these actions because the delinquent taxpayer failed to pay the taxes owed on the property over a set period ranging from two to four years.

The critical factor of these sales is that the taxing authority is abolishing only the interest of the previous owner and the rights of other interested parties holding liens or interest in the property will remain intact.

> An investor purchasing the deed at this type of sale is essentially taking the position of the original owner of record.

What this means to you as an investor is you are not only acquiring the deed to the property in question but also the obligations, agreements and encumbrances held against the property by other parties.

This would include taking the responsibility for the requirement to pay recorded mortgages, judgments held against the property and other costs that were incurred by the previous owner and secured against the property.

This scenario might put investment dollars at risk. The knowledge you are obtaining throughout this program regarding research of the title position of each property will enable you to assess the investment potential of each property. This ability to assess the potential of the property being sold enables you to bid on those offerings that provide the greatest return potential.

- Some of the property being sold at the subject to sale will actually be free and clear and adequate research will show you that there are no liens or other encumbrances recorded against the title to the property.

- Other property offered at this type of sale may have minimal liens and other matters that make the payment of existing title blemishes a wise choice for an investor.

- Some of the property being offered at the upset sale may be so heavily encumbered that the potential value of the property is already taken by other parties. These encumbrances leave little room for an investor to make a profit.

Conducting adequate research within the public records pertaining to the property will enable you to determine which category each potential investment falls into and bid accordingly.

The subject to sale can be one of the most exciting, profitable and least attended sales you will find within the tax sale-investment arena.

Many investors fear this type of sale because they are uncertain how to conduct a comprehensive search into the status of the title to the investment they are considering.

This fear on the part of other investors who lack the knowledge you are gaining through this coursework presents and incredible opportunity for you.

By using the search criteria, you will learn in the following chapters, you have an ability that most of the competing investors attending the subject to sale do not.

- You will have the fundamental knowledge that will enable you to approach the subject to sale confidant that you understand the status of each property on your bidding list.

- You will be able to place your bids and obtain the best offerings available at the sale feeling secure in the knowledge that your investment will provide you with the position and the return you desire.

The information pertaining to title research that is detailed in the coursework is essential to your success at tax sale investment regardless of the type of sale you are attending; however, the upset sale makes the education you are gaining invaluable to achieving your success.

The search techniques and training incorporated into your coursework is essential when preparing for this type of sale. You must complete an investigation into the condition of the title in order to secure your investment dollars when bidding at a subject to sale. This investigation is also known as an abstract of title and is the history, in chronological order, of a title from the initial government grant to the present ownership.

If you plan to attend a subject to sale, you should review the parameters you must research in an effort to complete adequate inquiry into your potential investments. This knowledge will enable you to understand the offerings at the sale in a way that many of the other investors in the room will be unable to do.

Rather than complete the search activity yourself, you may retain the services of an attorney or an abstractor to research each property you are considering. However, this can become a costly endeavor and will result in a lowering of the overall profits you will receive from your investment. You should carefully consider your investment strategy to determine whether investing the time required to conduct the research yourself will be more profitable for you than the payment required by a local abstractor.

Regardless of your plans pertaining to the most profitable approach, conducting adequate research will enable you to determine which offerings at the tax sale can return an incredible profit for you as the investor.

Certificate Sales

A tax lien certificate is a legal document representing unpaid real property taxes, non Ad Valorem assessments, special assessments, interest accumulations and related costs and charges issued in accordance with the applicable statute against a specific parcel or real property.

The tax certificate lien is created when a property owner fails to pay their real estate property taxes and other assessments as dictated by statute.

During the time the property owner is not paying the taxes due, penalties and interest accumulate on the initial assessment balance.

When the taxes remain unpaid for the specified period, the taxation authority creates the lien in an attempt to collect the monies needed and owed.

The tax lien certificate is the item being offered to investors during the tax lien sales.

- You can benefit through the purchase of the tax lien assessment due to the accumulation of the interest and penalties above the original tax assessments.

- The taxing body benefits when you purchase the certificate because they obtain the money owed to them for the operation of schools, police, fire, hospitals, etc. immediately upon your purchase.

As we discussed earlier, real property taxes usurp the priority of time with regard to the order of payment for liens. The order of recordation and wording of liens typically dictate the priority of a lien with regard to payment requirements. When a taxing authority places a lien against a property, this order is nullified in favor of the government taxation. The items detailed as part of taxing authorities unpaid monies become a first lien against the property against which they have been assessed. They are considered superior to all other liens held against the property regardless of the order in which the liens were placed.

Tax liens always take priority regardless of the order of time of recordation or priority wording incorporated into the security instrument of the other liens in existence.

The processes of the actions leading to a tax lien-certificate sale and methodology of the sale itself will vary by State and specific Jurisdiction. The details of these variations are explained later in the coursework, now you must understand what is being offered to you, as an investor, at the tax lien-certificate sale. In most States, the processes taken before the sale are much the same as those followed in the tax deed sales. At this type of sale, a tax certificate or certificate of sale is issued to the highest bidder rather than an actual tax deed.

The lien certificate is issued to the highest bidder in the amount of the unpaid taxes plus the interest and penalties allowed by Statute.

The certificate provides the investor with the rights to collect all of the taxes, interest and penalties incorporated into the lien.

In other words, the successful bidder for the tax lien certificate will pay the face value of the taxes and then collect all of the initial investment plus all allowable interest and penalties accumulated on that face value investment.

Some States will set the minimum bid required at the sale equal to the amount of the tax lien and allow the investor to bid up the pricing of the certificate until one successful bidder remains. In other States, the bidding will be based upon the rate of return that the investor is willing to accept on the investment. The face value of the certificate typically remains for lien regardless of the final bid on the certificate.

The successful bidder for the certificate will gain the right to collect any penalties allowed by Statute and Jurisdictional decree. These penalties would be assessed above the face value of the certificate.

All States that sell tax lien certificates allow for the accumulation of interest on the unpaid amounts. This potential interest accumulation is typically higher than what can be gained through placement of your investment funds in other opportunities. A chart detailing the current basis rate is included later in the coursework; however, the highest base rate does not always provide the best possible investment.

It is important that an investor in real estate think beyond the obvious. It is this ability to look beyond what is readily apparent that creates the difference between a decent investment and an incredible opportunity. Those investors that reach millionaire status typically have the ability to look beyond the basics and consider the unusual. This is one such situation. Many investors will flock to the tax certificate sale that offers the highest obvious base interest rate. These investors will readily bid against each other despite the fact that every bid raises the amount that they will ultimately pay for their investment.

It is imperative that you remember that the tax certificate you receive will usually remain at the face value despite the final bid at the sale. Every dollar above the face value that you bid for that certificate reduces the rate of return you can expect for your investment.

Example: Face	Value	$2500
	Initial Interest Rate	25%
	Expected Return	$ 625

This return is exceptional and would be difficult for an investor to match in another investment arena. This potential return on the investment dollar makes tax certificate investing an incredible opportunity for any investor. Now consider that you must gain the return in order to meet your profit calculations. Since there are many investors who will attend the same tax lien sale as you the rate of return you will achieve may not be the rate of return advertised for the sale. Many investors approach tax certificate investing following the obvious, the higher the rate of return allowed, the higher the ultimate profit. This is not necessarily true. If these investors bid against each other, the final rate of return on the certificate will decrease accordingly. Each decrease will reduce the return you will receive.

Example:	Face Value	$2500.00
	Advertised Rate	25 %
	Expected Return	$ 625.00

Bid Down Rate   12.5%
Actual Return $ 312.50

The actual return in the example is a tremendous reduction compared to the advertised return you expected to receive from the sale. If you review the rate applicable in other certificate States, you may locate one that offers a decent return rate while drawing fewer potential bidders. This lack of potential bidders will increase the likelihood that you will obtain the posted rate of return as compared to a highly attended sale where the bidder's activity will lower the return you can achieve.

The allowed, collectable interest rate is set by statute or jurisdiction and can range from 18% to 50% depending on the state in which you are conducting your investment activity.

The original property owner or anyone else who has a valid lien and interest in the property may redeem, or pay off the costs of this certificate from the sales high bidder. When the interested party pays the certificate costs, you obtain the expected return on your investment, including any penalties and interest accumulations allowed by Statute.

This payment must occur within the period set by statute or jurisdiction known as the redemption period. The interest accumulation and redemption periods by State are addressed later in the course.

If an interested party does redeem the certificate, the high bidder holding the certificate receives his investment plus any interest accumulations from the redeeming individual or entity in exchange for the certificate.

If the certificate is not redeemed or paid in full before the expiration of the redemption period the tax certificate may then become a tax deed giving the high bidder actual ownership of the property.

The owner of the tax certificate should apply for the deed and proceed with the proper foreclosure and/or eviction process as set for that jurisdiction to obtain entry right to the property.

Tax lien certificate-sales offer an incredible opportunity to gain an interest rate that is difficult, if not impossible, to obtain in other investment opportunities. A perceptive investment strategy will incorporate certificate investment into the final plan. The incorporation of certificate investments into your portfolio may enable you to gain the extra component that will ensure investment success!

REDEMPTION

Each state that uses tax certificates to collect the money owed sets a specific redemption period. Some of the tax deed sales also provide for a period of redemption following the sale. During this period, the owner in default on the applicable tax payments is given the opportunity to correct or redeem the property title by full payment of all monies owed.

If the certificate or deed is not redeemed within the set redemption period, the investor may proceed with any applicable action to collect the property that is pledged as security against the tax debt.

The waiting period or period of redemption varies by state and by the type of sale being conducted. Each type of redemption carries with it considerations beyond the simple obtainment of the funds you desire.

1. Some states allow for no period following a judicial sale for the owner to redeem the property title. This means that in a judicial tax sale, the sale is final and the owner may not act to regain the property from the investor unless this action is a private sector sale or transfer.

   This type of sale is usually a deed sale. This type of sale would rarely occur in a certificate purchase transaction since the purpose of making an investment at a certificate sale is often to obtain a return through the redemption. When you receive a deed at a sale that offers no post-sale redemption, you may immediately begin the process of gaining possession of the property.

   - Gaining possession means obtaining actual entry to the property.

   - A tax sale is different from most other real estate transactions in that no keys will be given to the new owner and the occupancy of the property will remain in question until the new owner takes steps to make this determination.

   The records search you conducted before the sale should have shown you any occupancy issues with which you must comply until you petition the courts for a removal of these non-ownership rights.

   Example: An occupancy issue that may exist is that of a life estate interest in the property. As the new owner, you must take legal action to remove this life estate interest or you must comply with the interest until it expires.

   Example: A common occupancy issue is a property that was leased to tenants by the previous owner. These tenants may have leaser rights in the property with which you must comply or that you must take legal action to abolish.

   The actual research you conducted when you physically looked at the property during your pre-sale research might have indicated such potential occupancy issues. Each situation or issue must be considered as part of your investment strategy. Some prior occupancy situations might be a benefit to the investor while others might create the need for an investment of additional time or money to remedy.

At times, an existing lease agreement might benefit the investor.

> If your investment strategy includes obtaining rental real estate, then obtaining ownership interest in a property that is already rented at the time of the sale will provide a ready source of immediate income from your investment.

If, however, you planned to renovate and use the property you gained at the sale as a primary residence, the occupancy by tenants could limit your ability to complete your investment plan.

Following this type of sale, it is best to proceed to the property to determine the actual occupancy status before making a decision with regard to your next steps. You should be aware of the probable occupancy status because of your pre-sales research. However, you will only be able to confirm such status with accuracy after you have gained an interest in the property.

2. Some states allow for 60 days or more for the redemption of an upset sale title. In an upset sale, the deed is being sold subject to the existing liens, encumbrances and other matters. In effect, the investor is taking the position of the original owner who failed to pay his taxes.

   This type of sale typically carries an additional post-sale redemption that allows either the original owner or other interested party to redeem the deed from the investor.

   You must wait for the redemption period to expire prior to gaining entry to the property and beginning the implementation of your plans for that property.

   Following this redemption period, all of the matters discussed in section one might exist. You will be required to take any additional steps necessary to free the property of non-owner type interests before you can gain entry to the property and begin making use of your new investment.

3. Tax Lien Certificate sales will typically carry a longer redemption period. This redemption period usually ranges from 6 months to 48 months or even longer in some cases.

   During this time, the original owner or other interested party may redeem the certificate from the investor. The certificate value continues to increase during this time because of interest accumulation so the longer an owner or interested party waits, the more value the certificate will gain.

Interest accumulation will vary by state and typically ranges from 18% to 50% depending on the jurisdiction in which the certificate was issued.

This is the cash return investment opportunity sought after by the investor who is looking for a liquid return on their funds.

It is important to note that this type of sale also carries the potential to obtain the deed. Obtaining the deed provides an interest in the property if the property owner or other interested party does not use the redemption period to make all applicable payments.

4. In some states, there are two different redemption periods.

There is a period that, once expired without the property owner making all payments as required, allows the investor to instigate a foreclosure proceeding.

> This foreclosure proceeding allows the investor to obtain a court order for the removal of all interest on the part of the defaulted taxpayer.

> In the event the investor does not choose to file a foreclosure proceeding, a later redemption opportunity may still exist. This opportunity provides the defaulted owner additional time within which to make payments as required.

> If the defaulted owner does not make the payments during this enhanced redemption period, the investor may then petition the court for the deed to the property. It is important that you gain awareness regarding the specific redemption terms of the sale you are attending. A tax lien certificate may expire and such expiration would leave the unwary investor with nothing except a piece of paper. The following chapters provide enhanced information regarding the redemption processes of the certificate investment. It is important that you gain a comprehensive understanding of your rights as a tax lien-certificate holder and the potential drawbacks to such a certificate before making any investment.

INTERESTED PARTY REDEMPTION

It is important, when considering this type of investment, to understand the individuals who can redeem a tax deed or tax certificate during the period of redemption. When you obtain a tax certificate the more individuals with the right to redeem the certificate the more likely, the redemption will occur and therefore the more likely you are to obtain the expected return on your investment.

The specific individuals who have the right to redeem the tax deed or certificate will vary by Statute and you should consult the applicable state in which you plan to invest for the final details pertaining to potential redemptions. The following section will provide you with an overview of the interested party redemption options you might encounter.

The individual against whom the taxes were assessed is provided with the opportunity to redeem his or her certificate or deed. This time is offered in an effort to ensure fair notification and opportunity for that individual to retain the rights and interest in his property. Statute or jurisdictional authority sets the term of redemption for these individuals.

A mortgage holder or other lien holder is provided the opportunity to redeem the tax certificate or tax deed because the taxation, foreclosure and sale procedures effectively negates or minimizes the lien holder's rights and interest in the property. This occurs because the taxing authority liens always take priority over other liens against a property. By redeeming the deed or certificate, the lien holder is then given the opportunity to regain their investment in the property through other methods of sale.

APPEALS

Another process may occur that would affect the investment you have made at a tax sale proceeding. This is the assessment appeals process.

The government retains the rights to divorce or take a property from the owner for the non-payment of assessed taxes as well as for a variety of other reasons. The other reasons are described in detail later in the course but are not as essential to the understanding of this section. The rights of the government to take ownership interest in real property from an individual are subject to very specific procedures that must be followed. These procedures are detailed and clearly defined and every step must be carefully followed to ensure the rights of the property owner are protected and that the fair practices as determined by statute are incorporated into the sale.

Often the process of notice by publication is the statutorily required notification to all owners or interested parties when a property will be appropriated for the purposes of tax collection.

The process of notice by publication is often a matter for appeal if the methods set forth by Statute are not followed exactly as set forth.

To determine if the service by process of publication was correctly followed in your jurisdiction requires an attention to the details set forth by statute. Some factors that must be considered are

- Whether statutory law empowers the court to proceed with the taking of the owner's interest and the subsequent sale of the certificate or deed

- Whether there are legal grounds for service of process by publication based on statutory provisions and judicial rules of practice

- Whether the affidavit of publication filed with the court conforms to the jurisdictional requirements

- Whether the court entered a proper order, establishing that the service by process of publication was satisfactorily completed

- Whether the notice was proper in its form, contents, and method of publication

- Whether the notice complied concerning placement of the notice for example in a newspaper

- Whether the notice was in compliance as to the time duration of the publication

- Whether, in addition to publication, there are additional notification requirements necessary to satisfy the statutory or judicial processes. These may include

  The posting of a notice at the courthouse

  The posting of a notice at the property to be sold

  A certified mailing of the notice to the residence of the owner of record of the property

  Other required notices as dictated by statute or jurisdictional regulation

- Whether all, some, none or additional requirements apply to property owners who are non-resident owners

- Whether personal service is required for the notice

The assessor or party permitted by court to conduct the sale typically ensures that the notices are delivered in compliance with all statutory and jurisdictional regulations before the sale is conducted. These cautions are included to provide you with an overview of the processes that should be followed. This does not mean that you must retrace the chain of notice for every property of interest to you. This does mean that a wise investor will research the history of the authorized body in terms of compliance in previous sales.

You might also investigate the specific regulations and the history of the taxing authority conducting the sale you plan to attend. A poor history by the taxing authority whose sales you are considering might be cause for reconsideration of your investment strategy. Your goal when attending the sale is to make an investment that will bring you a desirable return. To spend your investment dollars on a particular property only to have the purchase reversed due to an error in notice could slow your investment strategy progress. This reversal means that those dollars served no purpose to you in the intervening weeks or months. Investment dollars should be achieving a return every day they are out of the hands of the investor.

POST SALE REPAYMENT PROCESS

Some tax deeds do not allow for a post-sale redemption period. The delinquent taxpayer may make the required payments of past due taxes and penalties up to the date of the sale but no redemption may be made to the taxing authority or the investor following the sale. This means that when a bidder is successful at the sale, they receive the tax deed free of any waiting period. The investor may immediately begin to make use of the property according to their particular investment plans and needs.

Other tax lien and tax deed sales allow the delinquent taxpayer a period following the sale in which they may redeem the certificate or deed issued to the investor. The ability to redeem the certificate or deed is set by statute and will be reviewed in a late chapter within the coursework.

- If a redemption period exists, the taxpayer may go to the government offices detailed within their tax notices to pay off the debt. This payment will include all items dictated by the sale including the face value of the debt, all processing costs accumulated against the debt, interest penalties owed to the investor and any other penalty allowed by statute.

  If not all of the funds due under the certificate are paid, the certificate is not considered redeemed. The investor holding the certificate will receive the funds paid but will not lose the rights to the certificate until ALL money owed by the delinquent taxpayer has been paid in full.

- Upon full repayment, a check will be issued to the investor and the lien or deed is cancelled. At that point, the delinquent taxpayer once again holds full possession of the property subject to any other existing liens or encumbrances and the investor is able to take their funds, including the interest received, and reinvest it in another forum, including another tax sale.

POST SALE PROCESS WITHOUT REDEMPTION

The purpose of the lien investment is to gain the return attached to the redemption and as such, lien sales always allow for a redemption period. Some deed sales enable the delinquent homeowner to redeem the deed following the sale while others provide for no post sale redemptions whatsoever.

The redemption parameters of the sale that you attend will dictate the exact handling of the investment after you have been confirmed as the high bidder.

CERTIFICATE SALES POST REDEMPTION

If you have invested in a tax lien certificate, which the delinquent property owner or other interested party has not redeemed, you may obtain full rights to the property in return for your investment. You must wait for the expiration of the redemption period set by statute.

If the delinquent taxpayer makes no payment during the fixed redemption period, you may choose to notify the delinquent taxpayer that you are willing to wait longer for the repayment of the funds owed to you.

- Many states have set a maximum redemption period that you may provide to the delinquent taxpayer. You many not extend the redemption period beyond this time limit or the tax lien certificate you hold may expire and become worthless to you.

- If you believe that the delinquent taxpayer will still make payment toward the face amount of the certificate, plus the interest and penalties you are owed and you have no desire to hold the actual deed to the property, extending the redemption period may provide the taxpayer with the extra time needed to gather the funds owed.

  If you choose to apply for the deed to the property at the expiration of the redemption period, you must apply for the deed through the courts.

  If you choose to apply for the deed to the property, you will start a legal action within the court to gain the deed. This action may take anywhere from 3 months to one year or even longer depending on the region in which you live and the ability to locate the delinquent tax payer.

  If you hold a lien certificate and choose to apply for the deed, you may have to pay off any other outstanding tax certificates. This requirement is set by statute and bears further investigation prior to making any investment.

  The application to the courts to convert the lien to a deed typically provides the delinquent taxpayer with the opportunity to redeem his or her property until the day the court hands down the final judgment. This payment will usually include the payment of all legal fees incurred during the court process.

  If the delinquent taxpayer does not redeem the property before the date the court hands down the judgment, the investor owns the property. This ownership will often be a subject to or upset ownership meaning that it is ownership subject to all other existing matters held against the property. For this reason, another title search may be desirable prior to

TAX LIEN AND TAX DEED SALES

petitioning the court for conversion from a lien to a deed. When investing in tax liens or deeds, you must consider the level of risk that you are willing to bear concerning your investment. If no redemption period exists following the sale, the search you conduct or have conducted during your investment investigation period will provide you with a good idea of the level of risk you are taking on with the investment of your money. When a redemption period exists, it becomes critical that you understand not only any existing matters or liens against the property, but also any new matters that may be placed against the property and for which you will be responsible if you eventually gain ownership.

DEED SALES POST REDEMPTION

Following any redemption period for a deed sale purchase, the investor will gain the rights to the property granted by the taxing authority.

During the redemption period, the delinquent taxpayer may make payment to the taxing authority and redeem the rights to the property. This period ranges from 0 months to 3 years following the sale and will be set by statute for the sale that you are attending. It is important that you understand the redemption period and when you will obtain specific rights to the property in which you have made an investment.

- If you have invested in a tax deed, you hold the full deed to the property secured by your investment. The rights of this ownership will vary depending on the type of sale that you attend.

  Upset Sale   You are stepping into the position of the previous owner. This will mean that you gain rights to the property subject to any existing lines or encumbrances held against the title and the taxing authority makes no guarantees as to this condition. You should always conduct or have conducted a search into the chain of title you are considering as an investment.

  Free and Clear   The free and clear sale is also known as the judicial sale. Prior to this type of sale, the taxing authority will complete a process known as a judicial foreclosure. This frees the title of the property from many forms of liens and encumbrances. It is important to remember that certain liens such as IRS liens may still exist against the property. Other matters may be brought against the property following the date of the judicial foreclosure process and these matters will not have been nullified during the foreclosure. You should have or cause to have a full title search completed on the property before making any investment so that you will be able to bid knowing the exact condition of the property title.

Following this type of sale, you will still be unable to give full, marketable title to the property in most cases until you have completed a process known as a Quiet Title suit. More information pertaining to the quiet title suit is included in a later chapter for you to review.

CHAPTER

2

The Taxation Process
Why Can I Do This?

Taxes are charged to homeowners across the country to assist the Local and State Government in funding the operations that they offer to the taxpayer. There will always be people who do not pay the taxes assessed on their real property. Individual owners may die without heirs or with heirs who are not interested in redemption. Financial issues arise that make people simply walk away from their real estate, divorce happens and at times neither spouse will choose to take on the obligations of the property, partnerships dissolve, in other words life happens. These and many other personal matters will create tax-sale investment opportunities for you.

T ax sale investment is a business that offers incredible opportunity and from which you will not be downsized. The opportunity presented through tax sale investment will not disappear as long as real estate taxes exist.

You, as an investor at tax sales, will be performing a public service of providing the county and schools in your area with the funds they need to maintain operations while performing the personal service of securing your future through the incredible profit that exists within the tax-sale investment arena.

It is important that you understand the risks inherent to tax sale investments and take all of the steps outlined within this manual to help offset those risks.

It is important that you create an investment strategy that enables you to obtain funds, invest them safely and realize the best possible profit from each and every tax sale investment you make.

It is also important for you to understand each chapter of this manual and use the knowledge you are gaining to assist you in purchasing your first investment. This first investment will help to round out the education offered through this training and provide you with a true example of the wealth offered in tax sale investment. The first investment you make may not be the best investment of your career, but it is an investment in expanded knowledge. Do your homework, calculate the risk you can bear, choose a property and buy something! Once you have completed the purchase process once, you will have gained the same knowledge and typically MORE knowledge than any competing investor in that auction room. Most people work their entire lives to do what you will be doing in the next few years. They work to create a stable present and comfortable future for themselves and their family. You WILL do it NOW!

Before entering the tax sale arena, you should review the activities and processes that have brought the property to the sale. We touched lightly on the taxation process and the possible results earlier in the course. To invest in a tax sale certificate or deed you must understand the factors that caused the investment opportunity to exist.

- The taxing authority generates a budget that enables them to determine the exact taxes owed on each piece of real estate within their area.

- These taxes are levied against the real property in the area by the authorized taxing authority.

- The owner of the real property fails to make the required payment to the taxing authority.

- Interest and penalties are accrued on the tax balance owed.

- The grace period or term of payment expires.

- The taxing authority petitions the court for a judgment against the property in the amount of the unpaid taxes, interest accumulations and any penalties allowed within the jurisdiction.

This judgment could result in either a tax lien certificate or a tax deed.

The form of judgment will depend on the region in which you are investing and the type of sale the taxing authority is preparing to conduct.

- Final notices are issued to the delinquent taxpayer dictating the terms under which they may make payment and retain their property and confirming the intent of the taxing authority to sell the interest at an upcoming tax sale.

- If the delinquent taxpayer fails to make payment as dictated within the notices, a court appointed official will conduct a sale that allows investors to redeem these tax lien certificates or tax deeds from the taxing authority.

- The taxing authority uses the funds provided by the investor to meet the budgeted needs of the county, schools and other services provided to the region.

- A tax lien-certificate investor will then collect all unpaid tax assessments and penalties on the certificate well as all interest accumulated.

The rate of interest will be determined by the venue in which you choose to invest.

Some States set the interest premium at a higher level then others.

This higher rate of return might make the investment more desirable. However, the higher rate might also create more bidding competition. This could drive up the initial investment you will make at the sale and lower the overall profit you can expect.

It might be more profitable to obtain a property for a lower bid amount with a lower interest penalty.

This determination is one that will be made by each individual investor and is one of the reasons that tax sale investing creates opportunities for many types of investors to profit using a variety of investing styles.

- The investor in a tax deed gains actual interest in the property from the sale.

Gaining actual interest in the property provides a potential for incredible returns since the amount paid will typically be based upon the real estate taxes rather than the assumed value of the property.

Some areas do conduct sales in which the bid requirements are based on assumed value or other methods of pricing but the offerings will always present a valuable opportunity and discounted purchase to the investor who completes the research necessary to know which property is the most valuable investment.

- The deed investor will gain the interest in the property of the owner whose rights were removed by the taxing authority. The rights granted to the investor under the tax deed will vary depending upon the type of sale being conducted. As we have discussed, the taxing authority issuing tax deed interest may offer two variations of the tax deed sale. The uses the investor may make of this property granted under a tax deed will depend on the type of sale under which the tax deed is granted.

- The tax lien-certificate investor will receive a certificate entitling them to collect the face amount of the taxes owed as well as all penalties and interest allowed under the laws of the specific sale.

- When the redemption period or the time allotted for the property owner to make good his debt to the investor by paying all principal, penalties, interest and other charges expires, the certificate or taxing receipt then converts to a full deed on the property.

  This redemption period will vary depending on the sale you attend.

    Some sales allow for no additional period of redemption following the date of the sale. This means you will receive the deed to the property immediately upon confirmation of the sale. You will gain the interest of the delinquent taxpayer and have the opportunity to make use of the property in the same manner as the delinquent taxpayer.

    Other sales allow property owners to contest the sale for a specified period causing the investor to wait for this period to expire prior to gaining the final deed.

    The certificate sale provides an extended period for the owner to redeem the certificate. In this type of purchase, the investor is typically desirous of the payment of the lien rather than gaining the deed. If your goal were a cash return on your cash investment, this extended redemption period would benefit your investment strategy by giving the owner additional time to accumulate the cash that he will need for redemption.

This overview of the tax process is a simplified version of the activities that will occur in the creation of a tax lien certificate or tax deed sale.

This simplified chart is available for quick reference as you are completing your investment strategy. The remainder of the chapter is designed to provide you with a more detailed view of what actually occurs in the taxation process and how these events lead to your ability to purchase a tax certificate or tax deed.

Property taxes are the largest single source of regular income for local government programs. Schools, fire, police, libraries, and other locally funded programs rely on the income generated from property taxes for their operation. In some States, the State government also receives specific revenue from property tax assessments.

The taxes assessed against the real property are called the Ad Valorem taxes. Ad Valorem taxes are taxes that are assessed and levied against real property according to the value of each piece of property. The higher the value of the property the higher the tax assessment against that property will be. The theory behind the Ad Valorem taxation is that the more expensive properties are owned by those more able to pay the taxes.

ASSESSMENT

The process of assessment by the local government begins with the preparation of a budget for the next taxation year. This budget includes the costs of all items that must be supported by the government for which funds must be generated.

The budget committee or individuals in charge of the budget creation then determine the source of the funds that will be needed.

Other methods of obtaining money beyond the taxation of real property are incorporated into the budget first. These might include income such as

> Sales tax
>
> State revenue allocations
>
> Federal allocations
>
> City income taxes
>
> Business licenses
>
> Other sources of income as is common by jurisdiction

The total expected income from these sources is subtracted from the total budget needs of the jurisdiction. The amount of funds still needed for the fulfillment of the budget needs is then allocated as funds that must be created through property tax assessment.

Example:	Total Budget Needs	2,420,000
−	Funds from peripheral sources	− 1,220,000
=	Total needed from property taxes	= 1,200,000

This process of determining source of income to fulfill budget needs is called the appropriation process.

Simplified Appropriation Process

1. The final figures necessary for the operation of all local services is determined.

2. The income expected from other sources is deducted from the total funds necessary.

3. The real property in the area is then assessed to cover any deficit required from the budget.

ASSESSMENT PROCESS

1. The taxing authority will begin the process of assessment by determining the value of the taxable property within its jurisdiction.

   To determine the value of a property the tax assessor typically appraises the value of each parcel within the jurisdiction to set the value of the land and improvements.

   At times, this task is contracted out to a certified appraiser or appraisal company. The process of appraisal varies from State to State.

   This appraisal process is often detailed, time-consuming, and costly. As a result, the appraisal process is not usually completed on a yearly basis.

   Note: The appraisal basis used for assessment may be outdated and thus the assessed value of the property you are considering may not indicate the actual value of the investment.

   In some states, the appraised value is determined as the estimated fair market value.

   The fair market value is the amount one could expect the land and improvements to sell for if offered in the open market.

This type of appraising method takes properties of similar size, use, location, and condition that have sold in the recent past in the open market and compares them to the subject property being assessed.

The sales price of the sold property is reduced for any deficiency found in the subject property and increased for any factor affecting the subject property that is deemed above that of the sold property.

The final tally is then considered the fair market value for the subject property. This process is also known as a Comparison Approach Appraisal.

2. In some states, the appraised value or fair market value is converted into another figure.

This figure is obtained by taking the value of the land, adding in the replacement cost of any improvements to the land, and then deducting a figure for depreciation based on the wear, age, and obsolescence of the improvements.

3. The next step in the taxation process is to establish an assessed value to the property.

In some states, the assessed value is set at the same figure as the appraised value.

Other states use a percentage of the appraised value to determine the assessed value.

The assessed value is the value against which the taxes will be calculated.

Whether the assessed value is set at the appraised value or at a percentage of the appraised value typically does not affect the amount of taxes an owner will pay on the property. The tax rate calculation is simply factored according to the assessment method to obtain a fair taxation for each property.

TAX RATE CALCULATION

Once the property value has been determined, the next step is to calculate the rate of assessment that will be used to fulfill the budgetary needs. To calculate the rate of assessment, the assessor adds together the value of all property that will be taxed within the jurisdiction. The figure illustrating the value of all property in the taxation jurisdiction is then divided into the budget deficit determined previously.

Example:	All property in County Assessment	$ 40,000,000
	Budget Deficit	$ 1,200,000
	Rate	1,200,000

divided by   40,000,000   =   .03

This means that to generate enough income to fulfill the budget needs the taxation must equal .03 cents on the dollar of value for each piece of real estate within the taxation jurisdiction.

To reverse the process and better illustrate how taxation meets the budget requirements you would take .03 and multiply it by the total valuation of property or $40,000,000. The figure obtained equals the budget needs.

Tax Rate .03 x   Assessed Values $40,000,000   = Budget Needs $1,200,000

If all of the property within the jurisdiction is taxed at the .03 cents on the dollar figure calculation and all taxes are collected as expected, the budget projections will be met. This means that the city, county and state can meet their expected obligations for the following year.

Following the calculations of the expected budget needs and the value of the property in the jurisdiction, the figure calculated against each property are levied in the form of a lien.

The levy might appear in your tax rolls in a variety of forms but the most common form for expressing a tax rate is the mill rate.

MILL CALCULATION

A mill rate is a tax rate expressed as mills per dollar of assessed value.

1 mill = $1/10^{th}$ of a cent.

A tax rate of .03 cents on the dollar would be expressed as 30 mills.

1 mill = $1/10^{th}$ of a cent   3 mills = .03 cents

The next step in taxation is to apply the rate to each piece of real property in the tax rolls.

Applying the rate to a property with an assessed value of 20,000 is a matter of multiplying the mills required, in our example 30 by the assessed value of the property.

Assessed Value $20,000 X 30 Mills   = $600 Assessed Taxes

This figure will be issued as the tax bill on the property.

The taxing authority issues a lien against the property for taxes due based upon the applicable calculations. This lien is removed if the taxes are paid by the taxpayer as expected.

In many jurisdictions, the assessor calculates the assessment figures as described but not all of the property owners pay the billing from the taxing authority. Since the budget and assessment calculations are based upon all property in the assessment area, the lack of payment on the part of some property owners creates a deficit in the budget. This deficit must be met for the taxing authority to meet all of the budgeted obligations for the following fiscal year. The need to meet the budgeted obligations leads to the tax sales you will attend.

If the taxes remain unpaid the lien issued at the time of the tax billing remains against the property until such time as the taxing authority takes actions such as the sale of the lien certificate, the foreclosure of the property or the sale of a the property deed at the tax sale.

We explained earlier in the course that tax liens always take priority over any other lien against real property. Typical order of liens is that payment is made in the order of recording unless a specifically written subordination clause is incorporated into the document. The ability of the taxing authority to usurp the order of priority means that the tax lien is always paid first if the property is converted to cash through any means.

The county commonly collects the taxes for all of the taxing authorities in the area. This would include school, city, county and any other tax assessments used to support services in that area. This avoids the duplication of tax billings to the property owner and maintains a constant record, in one location, as to the status of tax billings and payments.

Taxes may be collected in a one-time payment per year but a more common collection method is to send two billings yearly. The first billing typically covers taxes due for the period from January 1 through December 31 of a tax year. The second billing usually covers taxes due for the period from July 1 through June 30 of the following year. Some States allow for a taxation discount if the payment due is made earlier than the due date on the bill. Nearly all states allocate penalties, costs, and interest if the payment due is paid later than the date of the bill.

Each State and Jurisdiction sets their own regulations for the time that is allowed to elapse before actions are taken beyond the norm to collect the money owed. The processes that will be followed with regard to these advanced actions do vary by State and, at times, by Jurisdiction within each State. The State-by-State guide will provide you with additional information regarding the actions that will be taken in your chosen investment arena.

CHAPTER

3

LISTS AND PROCESSES

The list of properties scheduled for an upcoming tax sale proceeding is typically published in one, some or all of the newspapers for a given jurisdiction. These lists will be published as soon as a determination of the properties to be included in the upcoming sale is made. This list may be subject to modification as the date of the sale nears. These modifications will occur as various owners redeem the property and therefore remove it from the upcoming sale.

I f the list is not published in the regional newspaper, you can usually obtain a printed copy of the list at the local county assessor or tax collection offices located at the county courthouse or applicable offices. These lists are copied versions of the property scheduled for sale and can usually be obtained for a small copy fee. Some counties now post lists on the Internet or make the lists available by mail. The potential availability of the lists will vary by State and by the specific County where the sale will be held. You should contact your county Tax Assessor's office to determine where you may obtain a list for the investment sale of your choice.

The lists are generated early in the proceedings and modified during the redemption period leading up to the sale.

These modifications will reflect properties that were scheduled for sale but were removed when a property owner or other interested party pays the required back taxes, penalties, and interest accumulations.

Statute or jurisdictional regulations make the determination of exactly what must be paid to remove the property from the schedule sale.

The period allowed for these payments is also outlined by Statute and Jurisdictional regulations. Some areas allow for the property taxes and penalties to be paid right up until the time of the actual sale.

The property that remains on the list after the redemption period has expired is the property that will be sold at the scheduled tax sale.

You may gain an investment interest through a tax certificate or an ownership interest through a tax deed by bidding on these remaining properties at the sale.

When the list is first posted, an investor should begin screening the potential properties that might be of interest them. It is important that you have alternate options available due to the late redemption and subsequent removal of some of the properties prior to the sale.

Given the depth of research required to secure your investment, it may seem reasonable to choose only a few properties as potential investments. This could prove disappointing if you arrive at the sale and discover that every property you researched was redeemed before the sale. It is possible that you will research many parcels and still have this occur, but each addition to your list lowers the probability that there will be no properties of interest to you remaining on the list when the sale commences.

Throughout the coursework, we have detailed to you the various research actions you will wish to take concerning your potential investments. Depending on the type of sale scheduled, different items may effect your position.

The taxing authority conducting the sale will advise you to conduct the research we have detailed in this coursework.

Each section of this manual contains vital items of research that you should consider completing prior to placing any bid at the tax sale. One such item is to locate the property you are considering as an investment.

An example of one instruction provided from the tax claim bureau is

Properties without street addresses may be located by comparing the map number with the property maps in the Assessment Offices. No guarantee or warranty is made, either general or special, nor as to the property lines, improvements or otherwise.

What this disclaimer means is that it is up to you, as the investor, to conduct sufficient research regarding the property listings to ensure you are purchasing a certificate or deed that will provide the best investment potential for you.

- To begin the process of elimination you should conduct or have conducted a thorough chain of title to the property in the public records system.

- You should also refer to the legal descriptions, assessors map books and the actual properties to ensure you have a thorough knowledge of the location of the property.

- You must locate any items within the public records, such as easements and access restrictions that may affect the property.

The research you conduct will assist you in gaining the knowledge of the property improvements, restrictions, locations and potential issues that may exist with regard to the property you are planning to purchase.

Before ever considering attendance and certainly before bidding at your first tax sale you should review this coursework to ensure you have obtained a comprehensive understanding of the research needs that will assist you in protecting yourself and your investment dollars.

To assist you in your research, each tax sale list published by the taxing authority will provide information that gives you vital insight into the property and key information you will use when conducting research into the property.

An example of an actual list published by a taxing authority is included on the following page. This is only an example and the lists you encounter when preparing for a tax sale may differ in some ways from the one that is included. Regardless of the form, the published lists will contain information from the county assessor's files that will assist you in the various aspects of your research.

It is your job to conduct due diligence research to ensure the information contained on the list is complete and that you use the information included on the list to protect your investment dollars.

The county assessor's office does not typically warrant the deeds they provide as to location, additional interested parties, or improvements to the land. It is up to the investor to conduct a sufficient search into the chain of title, to locate the property and to determine the existence or lack of improvements to the land.

Every section of this manual has detailed items of research about which you should have been making notes. The next chapters deal specifically with the items of research that are most critical to the tax sale investment processes. These items will prove valuable in screening potentially poor investments from those that will provide you with the return you desire. The creation of a strategy and the addition of research activity that will assist you in determining which offerings fit into your strategy is what will ensure you gain the desired return from every investment you make at real estate tax sales.

District	Control No.	Map No.	Owner Name	Property Location	Current Assessment	Fair Market Value	Transfer Tax	Deed Prep. & Recording Fee	Upset Price
140	39617	1400-22A-2-53 TR	XXXXXXXX	1655 Notre Dame Rd	$1,028.00	$12,541.60	$0.00	$25.00	$548.83
140	42918	1400-22A-1-40	XXXXXXXX	1649 EPI Valley Blvd	$375.00	$4,575.00	$91.50	$66.50	$384.46
140	36472	1400-23-15A	XXXXXXXX	1716 EPI Valley Blvd	$540.00	$6,588.00	$131.76	$66.50	$435.63
140	49927	1400-22-2 MIN	XXXXXXXX	206 Albright Dr	$1,185.00	$14,457.00	$0.00	$25.00	$942.79
140	21183	1400-22-2	XXXXXXXX	104 E Temple Ln	$1,170.00	$14,274.00	$285.48	$66.50	$725.88
140	50541	1400-23-6-4-4	XXXXXXXX	500 S Dartmouth	$1,170.00	$14,274.00	$285.48	$66.50	$719.88
140	49626	1400-23-9C	XXXXXXXX	124 Winston Dr	$3,675.00	$44,835.00	$896.70	$66.50	$1,120.87
180	25411	1800-03-90	XXXXXXXX	436 W Main St	$818.00	$9,979.60	$199.60	$66.50	$700.64
190	25717	1900-18B-9	XXXXXXXX		$2,618.00	$31,939.60	$638.80	$66.50	$3,358.14
200	27524	2000-04-21	XXXXXXXX		$1,125.00	$13,725.00	$274.50	$66.50	$716.54
200	40507	200-05-A1	XXXXXXXX		$2,385.00	$29,097.00	$581.94	$66.50	$1,465.28
220	30510	2204-07-48-A	XXXXXXXX	1350-52 Blair Ave	$4,103.00	$50,056.60	$1,001.14	$66.50	$2,174.63
220	50594	2207-12-1 TR	XXXXXXXX	58 Logan Ridge Vil	$2,078.00	$25,351.60	$507.04	$25.00	$1,331.65
220	30753	2204-07-34	XXXXXXXX	1317 Blair Ave	$195.00	$2,379.00	$47.58	$66.50	$6,793.39

Figure 3:1 – Sample Public Notice Sale List

Throughout the time while you are conducting your research, you should obtain updated lists of the property scheduled to be sold at the upcoming tax sale. These updated lists may allow you to remove specific potential investments from your list of possibilities. Obviously, continuing to conduct research on a property that has been redeemed by the owner and will therefore not be offered at sale would be a waste of your valuable time.

A consideration that many investors forget is that a property that you remove from the list of your potentially desirable investments today may appear at a sale in the future.

- Often a property that is redeemed once will appear on the list again in the future.

- At times, a property that appears at a subject to sale with too many liens to make it a desirable investment, will appear in the future at a free and clear sale.

As an investor, you will want to maintain a database incorporating all property for which you have completed research. At times, this incorporation into a master database will save you future research efforts by enabling you to eliminate property that you know from previous research was not a desirable addition to you portfolio. At other times, knowledge of the location and improvements on a property that you had eliminated as carrying too much debt load to be profitable may benefit you if those debts are abolished through the completion of a judicial foreclosure. The keeping of a database for use in the future may seem like an onerous task now, when you are attempting to learn the entire tax sale-investment process, but the potential returns in future savings of time and effort will make these efforts an invaluable addition to your investment strategy.

At this point, you may be wondering if it would be beneficial to wait until the sale is closer and the bulk of redemption's have occurred before beginning to research the possible investments. This appears to be a valid point until you consider the depth of research you should be conducting in order to secure your investment dollars. One of the errors that an investor might make is to enter the sale without all of the information they need to make a wise investment decision. By waiting until a late point in the process to begin researching your investment possibilities, you run the risk of not having adequate time to complete all of the needed research. Some investors have made the mistake of skipping portions of the research suggested in this course. These same investors often purchase property that turns out to be essentially valueless.

It is vital that you remember tax sale investments present an incredible opportunity for the investor who creates a strategy, puts forth the effort needed both before and after the sale and is intelligent and controlled in their bidding and buying decisions. However, tax sale investment presents many pitfalls for the investor who attempts to take short cuts when choosing property and walks into the sale unprepared without adequate information or a sound investment strategy.

The final list you obtain from the tax offices on the day of the sale will include any properties that have not been redeemed by the owner or other interested party during the period of redemption. Some jurisdictions do allow for the owner of record to make payment against the lien up until the actual commencement of the sale and the individual in charge of conducting the sale will typically make an announcement of any late redemption activity during the opening announcements period. Barring any late redemption activity, the list you receive when you enter the sale will be the final listing of the property available for purchase. It is advisable to arrive at the sale early so that you may compare the final list with your investment plan and make any alterations that you must in order to gain the property you desire.

Even with the possibility of late redemption, it is wise to obtain a listing late in the day on the last full redemption day prior to the scheduled sale. This list will allow you many opportunities to finalize your choices, set maximum bids, and enter the tax sale prepared and confident that you are ready to make your first investment.

The published notice announcing the upcoming sale and detailing the property that will be available will also provide the expected date of the sale. Knowledge of the planned sale date enables you to create a research timeline that will ensure all of the needed research activity is complete before the date of the sale.

The sale date will rarely be moved forward in time, in other words, the sale will rarely be set for a date earlier than the first posted date you see in the listing. Since the sale would rarely be moved forward in time, you can use the date published with the first list as a basis for the creation of your research timeline.

The sale date may sometimes be moved backward in time, in other words, the sale may be delayed. The impact of a delay in the date of the sale on your investment strategy is twofold.

1. In the event of a sale date delay, you gain additional time beyond your expectations to complete your research. This is a benefit in that it does allow you to complete a more comprehensive search into each possible investment.

2. The second effect of an alteration in the planned date is that if the date is adjusted backward, the owner's of record are provided with additional time in which to redeem their liens prior to the sale. This might minimize the offerings that are actually available on the date of the sale.

The final list published for the upcoming tax sale will typically contain some specific instructions regarding the process and terms of sale. You will also receive a copy of these instructions when you complete the registration process for bidding at the sale itself. An example of a series of final tax sale instructions is contained on the following pages. These examples have been extracted from the notice at an actual sale and should prove similar to the notices that you will see for your chosen tax sale.

DEED SALE – JUDICIAL SALE

To all owners of property described in this notice and all persons have interest in said property

Notice is hereby given by the TAX CLAIM BUREAU in and for the COUNTY under ACT _____ as amended, that the said bureau will expose at public sale in meeting room _____ prevailing time on DATE, or to any day to which the sale may be adjourned, re-adjourned or continued, for the purpose of collecting unpaid taxes, municipal claims and all costs incident thereto, including costs of recording deeds and all property transfer taxes, the following described real estate for at least the upset price in the amount herein approximately set forth.

In accordance with ACT, prospective purchasers at all tax sales are now required to certify to the Tax Claim Bureau that they are not delinquent in paying real estate taxes and municipal utility bills.

The sale of this property may, at the option of the bureau, be stayed if the owner thereof or any lien creditor of the Owner on or before the date of sale enters into an agreement in the manner provided by said Act, and the agreement to be entered into. Properties may be redeemed prior to the date of sale, by full payment of tax claims and costs. Otherwise, all sales are final.

The bidding will begin at the desecration of the bureau. All properties will be sold to the highest bidder. An attempt has been made to divest all record liens so that the property may be sold free and clear of all tax and municipal claims, mortgages, liens, charges and estates of whatsoever kind except ground rents separately taxed. The purchaser, at this sale, shall take and thereafter have such title to the property sold in accordance with the Act and pursuant to the Order of the Court.

Terms of Sale: No personal checks will be accepted. Payment may be made by Cash or certified check payable to the Tax Claim Bureau only.

Other conditions will be made known the day of the sale.

Figure 3:2 – Sample Public Sale Notification – Judicial Sale

DEED SALE – UPSET SALE

To all owners of property described in this notice and all persons having tax liens, tax judgments or municipal claims against such property:

Notice is hereby given by the TAX CLAIM BUREAU in and for the COUNTY under ACT _____ as amended, that the said bureau will expose at public sale in meeting room _____ prevailing time on DATE, or to any day to which the sale may be adjourned, re-adjourned or continued, for the purpose of collecting unpaid taxes, municipal claims and all costs incident thereto, including costs of recording deeds and all property transfer taxes, the following described real estate for at least the upset price in the amount herein approximately set forth.

In accordance with ACT, prospective purchasers at all tax sales are now required to certify to the Tax Claim Bureau that they are not delinquent in paying real estate taxes and municipal utility bills.

The sale of this property may, at the option of the bureau, be stayed if the owner thereof or any lien creditor of the Owner on or before the date of sale enters into an agreement in the manner provided by said Act, and the agreement to be entered into. Properties may be redeemed prior to the date of sale, by full payment of tax claims and costs. Otherwise, all sales are final.

The bidding will begin at the desecration of the bureau. All properties will be sold to the highest bidder. IT IS STRONGLY URGED that prospective purchasers have an examination of the title to any property in which they may be interested. Every reasonable effort has been made to keep the proceedings free from error. However, in every case, the Tax Claim Bureau is selling the taxable interest and the property offered for sale by the Tax Claim Bureau without any guarantee or warranty whatever, either as to structures or lack of structures on the land, liens, title or other matter or thing whatever.

Terms of Sale: No personal checks will be accepted. Payment may be made by Cash or certified check payable to the Tax Claim Bureau only.

Other conditions will be made known the day of the sale.

Figure 3:3 – Sample Public Sale Notification – Upset Sale

CHAPTER
4

RESEARCH

UNDERSTANDING REAL PROPERTY INCLUSIONS

One of the most vital keys to your tax sale success is to understand fully the nature and description of what is meant by real property. You must obtain a comprehensive understanding of real property so that you are certain you understand exactly what you are purchasing or investing in at the tax sale.

W hen you make a purchase of a piece of property, you are buying more than just a piece of land. The purchase of real property may include the fixtures, improvements, and land as well as specific rights as to the uses of aspects of the land. The items included with the purchase of real property are referred to as the bundle of rights and you must understand what portion of this bundle is being offered to you before you can determine the value of the investment.

In order to make prudent decisions pertaining to a tax sale purchase, you must determine exactly what portion of the full bundle of rights is being offered to you at the sale.

- You must gain a comprehensive understanding of what is meant by real property.

- You should cultivate the ability to review deeds and other records to determine what inclusions or limitations might effect your investment.

- You must gain an understanding of the coding used by a particular taxing authority that indicates what rights are being transferred.

When you have gained all of the base knowledge incorporated into this course, you will be able to feel secure that you are purchasing the exact interest in the real property available at the sale that you expect.

Example: At a recent sale we attended, an individual who did not fully understand the nature of real property did not conduct an adequate inquiry into the tax sale investment they were making.

He bid on multiple 'parcels' available at the auction.

The total cost of these 'parcels' was nearly $10,000.

Unfortunately, the investor did not realize he was buying only the mineral rights to these acres of land.

The investor thought he was investing in the land itself.

If the investor had made an adequate search into the public records, it would have been obvious that the mineral rights to the property had been transferred by contract. He could then have compared the mineral right contract holder's name to the name on the tax sale listing forms.

The owner of record whose interest was abolished by the sale was the owner of record for only the mineral rights to this land.

This is an example of only one of the disappointing and expensive mistakes that can be avoided if a solid knowledge of real estate fundamentals is gained before implementing a tax sale, investment strategy.

Other potential pitfalls await the investor who does not learn the basics of real estate and the rights that may be severed or included with a purchase. The potential pitfalls for the investor who does not make an adequate attempt to research potential investments prior to placing his bid are innumerable. Some common errors in bidding that you may see other investors would include

- The purchase a property with the plan of using it as a primary residence or rental property only to discover that it does not contain improvements or contains only condemned improvements.

  The lack of improvements would minimize the value of the investment.

  The condemnation of an improvement could require that the investor spend additional funds to either restore the improvement to remove the condemnation or tear down the improvement leaving the investor with only the land.

- The purchase of a tax certificate believed to be secured against a well-developed and valuable piece of real estate only to discover that the tax certificate is only secured by the mineral rights of that land.

  It is possible that the delinquent taxpayer holding the mineral rights will redeem these rights prior to the expiration of the redemption period, but it is less likely than if the certificate is held against the land and improvements.

  If the delinquent taxpayer does not redeem the certificate during the redemption period completing a foreclosure process on only the mineral rights of the land might not be beneficial or profitable for the investor.

- The purchase of a building lot with the strategy of turning the land over on the general market to quickly gain additional capital only to learn that easements effect the land making it virtually impossible to improve under zoning ordinances.

  The investment in this land would be essentially valueless, as the parcel cannot be used. This would make the capital investment a loss for the investor.

- The purchase of a solid appearing house with the intention of performing basic aesthetic functions and then using the building as a rental or capital building flip property only to learn that this property carries water liens, mechanic's liens, mortgages and other encumbrances that sap all possible equity that may have existed.

These are only examples of common tax sale-investment errors that may be made by the unwary investor. Each of these errors could have been avoided through competent and adequate research into the potential investment.

By gaining a solid foundation of knowledge that allows you to research your potential investments before you risk your money, you can avoid the common pitfalls of tax sale investment and securely place your investment dollars to reach for your dreams.

By obtaining a comprehensive understanding of the taxation process, the tax sale lists, real property and the ownership interests in real property that can exist as well as liens, encumbrances and other title defects you may encounter, you will have the ability to choose your investment wisely. This will enable you to protect your investment dollars and assist you on the path to success.

The following sections will provide you with a comprehensive understanding of what is included in real property transactions as well as the possible methods that may have been employed in the dividing of the rights to the portions of real property. It is essential that you complete the fundamental sections of this course before moving into the tax sale, investment arena. These sections will enable you to fully research your investment choices and allow you to feel secure in the knowledge that your investment will provide you with exactly what you expect.

Real property includes the land and land carries additional rights.

Each investor will have different ideas regarding the best investment opportunity for their portfolio.

- Your strategy might dictate that you purchase only sub-surface or mineral rights.

- Your strategy might also dictate that the best investment for you is the one that carries an intact bundle of rights.

The determination as to whether an offering at the sale will fit comfortably within your investment portfolio can only be made once you have determined exactly what is being offered. To make this determination you must clearly understand the rights included with real property and the records that will indicate to you the status of these rights.

Surface rights   Surface rights include anything that is on the land, or permanently attached to the land and can be numerous. These rights must be most scrutinized during your research, as they are the most commonly restricted rights you will encounter. A complete section devoted to surface rights is included on the following pages.

Sub-surface rights   Sub-surface rights include anything that is below the land such as coal, water, ore, mineral deposits, etc.

Sub-surface rights are typically included in the bundle of rights during a real estate transfer.

Subsurface rights include the rights to the space and natural resources that are contained to beneath the surface of the earth of the property being conveyed.

The term sub-surface right is defined as the right to all or certain specific natural resources that lie beneath a parcel of land.

Sub-surface rights typically include the right to enter beneath the surface of the land explore the area beneath the surface of the land for natural resources and extract the natural resources from the land .

Mineral rights are an example of an inclusion within the term subsurface rights.

Sub-surface resources are subject to the same rights of ownership as any other portion of the land.

> The right of ownership to these resources may be severed from the overall bundle of rights.
>
> This severance may cause additional taxation.
>
> When you invest at a tax sale, it is important to remember that you might be bidding on the surface rights, sub-surface rights, air rights, or a combination of these three rights.

It is important that you make adequate inquiry into the public records to determine what rights are intact with regard to the property you are considering. The severance of a resource right may be completed through a variety of methods and it is important that you review any document that pertains to the bundle of rights. You should review the records pertaining to the property you are considering paying specific attention to

- Conveyance or grant document

- A lease of the named rights

- A mortgage against the minerals

- Adverse possession

- A contract between parties that pertains specifically to the resources

- A judicial determination

If any of the documents listed above or additional documents that are not named are in existence concerning the property you are researching, it is vital that you fully review each document. You must determine the status and transferability of these specific rights.

Sub-surface right severance allows different owners to hold title to different resources that belong to the same parcel of land. In addition, the severance of resource rights may affect the rights of ownership for the property you are researching.

Any severance of sub-surface rights must be noted so that you may conduct additional research at the taxation offices to determine which rights are being offered at the upcoming sale.

Air Rights

Air rights include anything that is directly above a particular parcel of land such as electrical wires, tree limbs and in most cases the actual section of air and atmosphere.

Generally, the rights to the ownership of a piece of land also include the rights to occupy and use the airspace above the surface of the land.

In real estate law, airspace is defined as a unit of real estate three-dimensionally described (L, W, H) created through the horizontal subdivision of the space existing over a particular tract of land.

It is important to remember that airspace is subject to conveyance and other forms of alienation the same as any other right included with the bundle of rights. Air rights are also subject to any matter, lien, or encumbrance that affects the land.

Possible transfers of airspace would include the sale of condominiums, walkways, and navigational easements.

A unit of airspace is commonly known as an air lot and is identified by both the parcel of land beneath the unit and the addition of the horizontal and vertical parameters of the unit or lot.

Airspace ownership is subject to

o   Federal regulations

o   Statutory provisions

o   Local government disposition

o   Zoning ordinances

    o   Private or individual restrictions or limitations

These restrictions and limitations are commonly found in the areas of navigable space, airwaves etc.

Real estate transactions that involve airspace and air rights are extremely complex. Any document that indicates a severance of air rights discovered during your research should be carefully reviewed. It would not be feasible to purchase a property with an air rights encumbrance if you plan to erect a high rise building on that land. The use of the air rights of a particular parcel might also lower the perceived value of that parcel.

Understanding the method of land parcel ownership is a vital key in the understanding of the air rights, surface rights, and sub-surface rights of a piece of property.

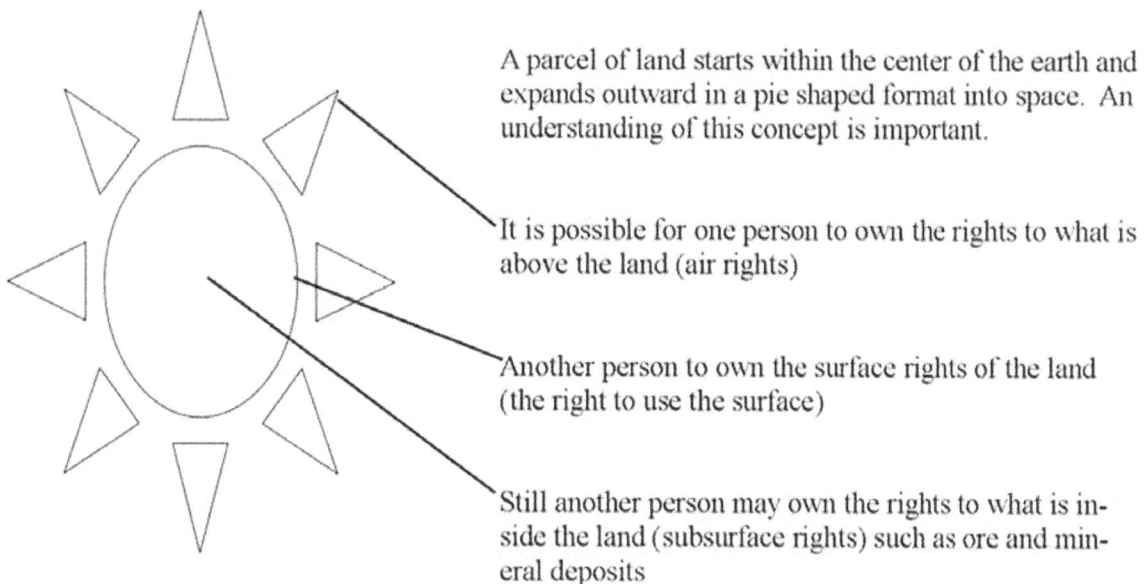

A parcel of land starts within the center of the earth and expands outward in a pie shaped format into space. An understanding of this concept is important.

It is possible for one person to own the rights to what is above the land (air rights)

Another person to own the surface rights of the land (the right to use the surface)

Still another person may own the rights to what is inside the land (subsurface rights) such as ore and mineral deposits

Figure 4:1 – Diagram – Real Property Rights

SURFACE RIGHTS

Surface rights are commonly referred to as the rights to the land and the improvements of the land. Most investors believe this is the actual item they are gaining rights to at the tax sale. It is true that this is the most commonly transferred interest and it is true that this is frequently the most valuable interest you can gain. However, the value of the surface rights can be impacted by the transfer of the other rights and can be severed in a variety of ways thereby limiting the potential of the purchase you are planning. A comprehensive understanding of surface rights is perhaps the most essential element in your tax sale investment strategy success.

Real Property surface rights include the improvements that exist that are actually affixed to the surface of the land.

The term real property includes anything affixed to the surface of the land. These are known as Improvements. Improvements may include

- Buildings, structures, pipeline, pavement, fences, etc

- An item of personal property that has been attached to the land might then become a real property

  Personal property affixed to the land in such a way that it is considered a real property improvement then becomes known as a fixture

- Trees, perennials, and vegetation on the land are also considered a part of real property. These are known as fruits of nature.

- Anything else affixed to the land that improves the value of the land is also considered part of real property

When a seller is selling a piece of real property, he or she is actually selling the rights that they hold to use all of the items that are a part of that property.

When the taxing authority sells a tax deed, they are transferring only those rights held by the delinquent owner whose rights are being removed through that particular sale. They are not necessarily transferring the full bundle of surface rights. If the owner of a particular tract of land has severed the bundle of rights from the whole but has not transferred the interest in those rights to another party, the taxing authority will tax those rights separately. If the property owner makes payment on one portion of the rights, that portion will not be sold at the sale. Only the portion of the rights for which the property owner is delinquent will be sold at the sale.

Example: A property owner severs the sub-surface rights to his property from the overall bundle of rights with the intention of selling the mineral rights to another party.

The property owner creates a lease agreement transferring the mineral rights.

The taxing authority taxes the rights separately because of the severance by the property owner.

The lease expires but the mineral rights retain their severed status.

The property owner is responsible for paying both tax billings on the property, those issued for the mineral rights and those billings issued on the remaining property rights.

The property owner makes payment for all of the tax billings received except those pertaining to the mineral rights of his property.

The taxing authority completes a judicial foreclosure leading to a tax sale conducted that transfers only the mineral rights.

You must conduct the research into the public records necessary to determine what rights the owner whose interest is being sold held.

The rights you receive in the purchase will be limited to only those rights held by the previous owner and being abolished through the sale. Any limitation that affected the delinquent owner's rights to the property will also affect your rights to the property and the potential uses you may make of the investment. These limitations could have dramatic impact on the profitability potential of the investment.

The ramifications of rights limitations when you purchase a deed at the tax sale are obvious. Every limitation placed upon you minimizes the potential sales price and uses of the property. The ramifications of limitations in a purchase at the tax-lien certificate sale are less obvious but could have an equally negative impact on your investment expectations. The fewer rights that the delinquent property owner is losing, the less likely the probable redemption and therefore probable return you can expect from the certificate.

FIXTURES

The items that are within the home that are categorized as fixtures are typically included in a real estate transaction.

A property sold at a tax deed sale is offered to the highest bidder on an as is basis. There are many ramifications to the as is purchase, but the one relating to fixtures dictates that the interest of the delinquent taxpayer in the property contents considered to be fixtures is abolished at the time the deed is transferred. The inclusion or exclusion of fixtures when considering the value of the real property you are purchasing can affect the value of an improved property.

A fixture is a piece of personal property that has been affixed, installed, or permanently attached to a parcel of land or the structures on the land.

If the piece of personal property is permanently attached according to the lawful description, the item then becomes a part of the real estate.

Since fixtures will affect the value you can obtain from your investment, it is important for you to gain an understanding of which items located on the property are considered part of the transaction following the sale. Four standards can be applied when determining if an item is considered a fixture.

1. The intention of the parties in the transaction

2. An agreement between the parties in the transaction concerning the status of the particular item in question

3. The manner in which the item is attached to the real property

4. The item itself and its adaptation to the real estate

Due to the methods you are employing to gain the property, you will probably not request an explanation from the owner regarding his intentions regarding the fixtures of the real property. However, you may locate agreements and other recorded documents during your public records search that allow you to infer the intentions regarding fixtures. A fixture named in a previous contract can be assumed to remain with the real property you are gaining at the sale. This is not always the case and actual inquiry at the subject property will be necessary. It is best to believe that the only items you will gain through your purchase will those you visibly observe. Many owners, when losing interest in real property through tax sale proceedings, will remove all possible items in an attempt to retain as much profit from their estate as possible.

Another issue may occur with regard to fixtures that may affect you after the sale. In some states, liens specifically placed upon fixtures are recorded in a specific manner that allows for the premise of constructive notice to have been served to any purchaser or mortgagor of the property.

This constructive notice would prohibit the transfer of this fixture despite the meeting of the four qualifications listed above. Certain tax sales complete a foreclosure process against the property prior to offering it for sale at the public tax sale. A foreclosure proceeding might not apply to a fixture used as security against funds borrowed. In this instance, you might be required either to redeem the funds owed against that fixture or to return the fixture to its rightful owners, the lien holders, in an acceptable condition.

Example: A built in appliance for which an outside company has provided financing might be considered a secured item.

The appliance acts as security against the funds provided for the purchase of the appliance.

The appliance would then be subject to a lien outside of the standard liens typically encountered in a tax sale proceeding.

A complete search of the public records pertaining to the property owner and the property itself should show you any recorded items that might affect the rights you will gain with regard to fixtures contained on the property.

If no notice is discovered during the search process, you can generally assume good title to fixtures that are affixed to the property in a manner that causes them to be construed as real property. This would allow you to sell, dispose of, or otherwise make use of the fixtures you discover in the property you purchase.

PERSONAL PROPERTY

If an item is classified as personal property, it will not be included in the sale of real property. Items that may fall under this category include:

- Detached furniture and appliances

- Business articles affixed to a rented building by a tenant

- Annual cultivated plants and crops

CROPS: It is common for the sale of a parcel of land to include any plants and crops that are growing on the land. At times, the crops growing on a parcel may be sold by contract and separated from the land.

- This separation may be completed by deed and may be taxed separately from the other portions of the full bundle of rights. As a tax deed investor, you should thoroughly investigate the public records pertaining to any land your purchase. If you locate a document providing rights to the crops of the land, you must also determine which portion of the bundle of rights is being offered at the sale. It is possible that you are purchasing only the crops located on an investment opportunity.

- It is also possible that you will purchase property that contains crops but that an individual other than the owner of record will own these crops. It is the owner of record against whom the taxing authority took action. This means the crops owned by another individual will not be a part of the transaction you are conducting. If another individual has rights, applicable to the crops on the land, the value of the property may be affected and you may be required to comply with any harvesting contracts applicable to the crops.

If you locate a specific contract negotiating the sale of crops, you should conduct further research into the tax sale lists to determine what interest is being sold. The taxing authority may be selling the interest in the real property or only the interest in the crops themselves.

You will also want to consider the impact the severance of this interest might have on the overall value of your investment.

OTHER PROPERTY

An important consideration when purchasing tax deeds is the personal property that may remain following your gaining an interest in the real estate.

The type of sale you are attending will dictate the disposition of personal property.

- Some statutes and particular jurisdictions provide you with the ability to dispose of the personal property immediately upon receipt of the valid purchase receipt for your new investment.

- Others require you make every attempt to return these personal items to the previous owner prior to disposal.

The taxation office where you are making your investment will be able to assist you in the specific handling requirements for abandoned personal property that remains in and on the investment following your purchase.

SEVERANCE OF RIGHTS

We have discussed the elements included in a transfer of real property. The previous pages have referred often to the severance of specific rights applicable in such transfers. It is critical to your investment that you understand the methods that might be employed to server specific land interest and apply this knowledge to properly researching each parcel to determine the rights you will gain if you purchase that property at the tax sale. The reasons for the severing of a specific right applicable to the land will vary by transaction.

- The severance of the improvements from the land may increase the value of the property.

- The severance may occur in an attempt to reduce the taxes placed upon the land.

- Severance may occur as part of a sale or leaseback transaction or some other technique used in the ownership or transfer of real estate that creates a financial benefit or perceived benefit for the involved parties.

- Severance may occur through the enforcement of a right by either a private or a public entity.

Jurisdictional law is applied to any transaction that severs the full bundle of rights and interest in the land. It is important to understand the terminology surrounding the various rights you may come across in your research.

A property's value is affected by its ability to provide full rights to the owner as well as by its size and shape. When you begin to conduct research, pertaining to a property offered by the taxing authority, you would typically only receive the lot description or tax id number from the tax lists. The dwelling or improvements to the land will usually not be incorporated into the lists. Since these items do affect the value of the property you should research all matters including the location, quantity of land, shape and the included rights of the parcel by reviewing all of the public records that reference the property investment being offered.

Any investment of your money requires as complete an understanding of what you are obtaining as possible. A section is included in a later chapter to assist you in understanding the descriptions of land you may encounter during your research. Determining if the land you are considering as an investment contains improvements and locating a particular tract of land by the legal description and by the assessor's maps and numbers is an essential element to your investment success.

CHAPTER 5

INTEREST LIMITATIONS

It is a large portion of your research function to determine exactly what parties may have obtained an interest to each right and interest of a particular piece of property. When you purchase a tax sale deed, you will be obtaining only those rights held by the individual against whom the taxation authority has taken action. Other individuals may retain specific rights in conjunction with your new purchase. When you invest in a tax certificate, you will gain an interest or lien against the property in tandem with the other parties who hold a specific interest.

The process of determining what individual might hold interest in the property and what limitations have been placed on the property requires an understanding of the methodology of estate interests. Throughout history, basic systems have been used to govern the granting of land.

- **Feudal System**   Under the feudal system, a king owns all of the land and he is responsible for providing protection to the subjects who inhabit the land. This system is typically not one you will encounter in the

United States. It is still used in certain portions of the world and the understanding of this system will enhance your overall understanding of the manifestations that have occurred to lead us to our present day system of land management.

- **Fee Tail**   A second system of estate interest known as the Fee Tail Estate was employed by the English Parliament to keep land ownership in the grantee family as long as a direct line of descent existed. A common name for this process is the process of entailment. This land governing methodology is rarely used within the United States. If you encounter the entailment processes within your research, it would be detailed as a restriction rather than applicable law.

    In this type of estate, the grantee is often referred to as a fee tail tenant. This fee tail tenant is limited as to the actions he can take regarding the estate. The fee tail tenant is often limited concerning the rights to burden, convey, mortgage or otherwise encumber the estate. These limitations on his abilities are put into place to ensure the estate remains within a family line.

    Today you might see similar limitations with regard to the use of the land. These limitations will be outlined in a specifically recorded document. This document could affect your rights as the new titleholder. More information regarding such restrictions is included later in the coursework.

- **Allodial System**   The system used within the United States is patterned as an Allodial System. Under the Allodial System, an individual can own all land. They own the land in absolute independence.

    The owner owes no rent, service, or allegiance to any government.

    There are many types of ownership interest under our current system.

    This system closely resembles the Allodial system but has a variety of categorical ownership types that need to be understood. The variations detailed in the following pages are the most common you will encounter and it is important that you understand the ramifications of each specific type of estate ownership specific you will encounter.

FREEHOLD ESTATE

A freehold estate is an ownership interest where one owns and possesses real property.

Ownership under a freehold estate is for an unspecified duration. A freehold estate continues until the owner knowingly relinquishes their rights and interest in the estate

- Knowingly relinquishing your rights and interests does include the failure to take actions such as paying real estate taxes.

- A failure such as the non-payment of real estate taxes or a mortgage lien may result in the taking of an owner's rights and interests in a manner that is not exactly voluntary but does result from an action taken (failure to act) on the part of the owner.

The concept of real estate ownership can be easiest understood when you view ownership as a bundle of rights or collection of rights to the ownership.

- The government retains the rights to taxation, eminent domain, police power, and escheat concerning real estate.

- All the other rights associated with real estate are granted to the owner.

  These are called fee simple rights and are available for private ownership.

  A person and his heirs can hold the fee simple bundle of rights for an unlimited amount of time.

LIMITATIONS IN THE BUNDLE OF RIGHTS

In addition to understanding the types of estates you may encounter, you should also understand the division of rights that may occur in real property. The level of interest one has in the Real Property is typically described as a bundle of rights. The bundle of rights refers to the collective rights of ownership interest in a property that can be held by the owner of the property or divided among a variety of owners.

When investing at the tax sale, you will purchase only those rights held by the owner whose rights are being abolished in an attempt to collect the taxes due against those rights.

It is important that you understand and research any limitations you may encounter in the investment you are considering. Limitations may affect both the use you may make of your property and overall value you can expect to receive if you sell the property in the future.

LIMITATIONS

The concept of real estate ownership is most easily understood when ownership is viewed as a collection or "bundle" of rights that may be divided among one or multiple individuals. The initial bundle of rights is split into two parts, the government's interest and the individual owner's interest.

The government retains the rights to

- Taxation

- Eminent domain

- Police power

- Escheat

All the other rights associated with real estate are granted to the owner.

- These are called fee simple rights and are available for private ownership.

- A person and his heirs can hold the fee simple bundle of rights for an unlimited amount of time.

Estate: The word estate is a synonym for bundle of rights.

Fee Simple: Fee simple estates are estates that may be inherited by ones heirs and assigns.

The fee simple estate refers to ones legal interest or rights in land.

Most real estate transactions are for the fee simple estate. In other words, when a person says he or she owns a piece of property they are typically discussing these fee simple estates.

The word title refers to this ownership. Any time someone besides the "owner" obtains a claim against a person's estate it becomes an encumbrance.

Encumbrance: An encumbrance is any claim, right, lien, estate, or liability that limits the fee simple title to a property.

> Commonly you will find encumbrances that are easements, encroachments, deed restrictions, liens, lease, and air and surface right restrictions.

When researching the title for investing in a fee simple estate it is important that you locate and note any encumbrance that may exist in the chain of title. These encumbrances may affect your rights to make full use of your new investment.

The removal of a "stick" from the bundle of rights or the imposition of a limitation of an owner's rights to the land can arise from either public or private sources. This removal limits the rights of ownership interest to the property. As an investor, you should understand that this removal will affect the value and potential uses of your new purchase.

GOVERNMENT LIMITATIONS

Government (public) limitations apply to all real estate and may come into effect at any time.

Police Power
These limitations may occur because of police power. This means the limitations are placed in order to protect the health, safety, and general welfare of the public.

Examples: Zoning laws

Condemnation of a property

The research of any standard and any specific use of police power should be included as an essential portion of your tax sale research process.

The zoning of a property can drastically influence its value.

The zoning of nearby property may also affect the value of your new investment.

If you gain actual interest in the real property, you must comply with any use of police power that affects that property.

If you gain a lien certificate against the property, the use of specific police power actions may influence the probability that the lien will be redeemed.

Condemnation
The government may create easements against the property. This is accomplished through a process known as government condemnation. An easement of this type can occur for a variety of reasons.

Example: A common government easement would occur when the government is acting to control a flood area and runs drainage pipe over or under the owner's property.

When a portion of the land you are considering has been condemned through proper procedure it is important that you gain this knowledge before your purchase.

Your ownership interest will be subject to the same acts of condemnation, easements, encroachments, and other matters as the previous owner of record. These limitations will affect the value of the investment and as such could dramatically affect the success of your investment strategy.

The probability that the owner of record will redeem the tax lien certificate can also be effected by how an act of condemnation or police power affects the owner's ability to make use of the property. The more limitations to the use of the property that exist, the less valuable the property becomes. The less value that the property holds for the delinquent owner, the less likely they become to make the required payments to you to redeem the certificate.

Escheat   The government may also gain interest in a property through the process of Escheat. Escheat occurs when an owner dies and leaves no will or heirs enabling the property to revert to the state for disposal.
The process of escheat may actually result in two assignments of the property that occur simultaneously.

- The taxing authority may conduct a sale in an attempt to gain the funds required under the tax lien placed on the property.

- The court may authorize the state to issue the interest held through the process of escheat to the heir dictated by statute.

If it appears that the statutes of descent will apply to the property, it is important that you make further inquiry through the courts to determine the status of the actions planned. Understanding the status of the actions that will effect the investment will enable you to determine if an heir exists, that will ultimately limit your interest in the property.

Taxation   All privately held property is subject to the government right of taxation. Governments finance themselves by requiring property owners to share the cost of the benefits they receive from the government. The currently employed method of real estate interest assignment enables the government to retain the right to collect property taxes from landowners. It is because of this right that you gain the opportunity to invest in tax sale deeds and lien certificates.

To ensure that property owners pay their real property taxes in the proscribed period, the right of taxation enables the government to seize ownership of real estate if taxes become delinquent. The government may then sell the property or generate a tax lien certificate to recover the unpaid taxes. The seizure of the delinquent property owner's interest by the taxing authority results in one of two opportunities for you as an investor.

- The government may abolish all of the interest of the delinquent property owner. This results in an offering of this interest at a tax deed sale and enables the investor to gain all of the rights held by the taxing authority.

- The government may create a tax lien certificate that enables the investor to pay the face value of the taxes owed by the delinquent property owner. Following the purchase of the certificate, the investor will gain the ability to collect all of the interest and penalties that would have been due to the taxing authority if the certificate had not been sold.

These seizure options assist the taxing authority in ensuring the expected revenue for the operations of the different functions that they provide to the public. These collection options also create the invaluable investment opportunity you are completing this coursework to understand.

Eminent Domain   Eminent Domain is the taking of a piece of private property for public use. The right of eminent domain is withheld from the bundle of rights by the government so that they may take ownership of privately held real estate for the benefit of the public regardless of the owner's wishes.

- The land may be taken for schools, roads, parks, urban renewal and other public and social purposes.

Other companies, which are partially public entities such as utility companies and railroads, are also permitted to obtain land using the processes of Eminent Domain.

- Eminent Domain may only occur with just compensation or payment for the taking of the privately held land.

- Eminent Domain occurs following a legal process called condemnation or a condemnation proceeding, in which the government condemns the portion of the land to which they require access or use.

- The property owner must be paid the fair market value for the property, which is being taken from him.

- The actual condemnation is usually preceded by negotiations between he property owner and an agent for the public body wanting to acquire ownership.

> If the parties can arrive at a mutually acceptable price, the property is often purchased outright.

> If the parties cannot reach an agreement as to the value and price of the land, a formal proceeding is filed against the property owner in a court of law.

> The court hears expert opinions from appraisers and then issues a ruling as to the price of the property.

- This condemnation may be for the entire fee simple estate or for an easement that grants rights to a portion of the estate, typically in the form of right to access or come through the property.

> When only a portion of a parcel of land is being taken for use severance damages may be awarded to the property owner. These damages are in addition to the payment for the land actually being taken.

It is important that you discover any actions of eminent domain, which may have occurred in relationship to the investment you are considering.

Only the property owner in possession at the time the condemnation occurs will typically be compensated for the loss of the land that occurs because of the act of eminent domain. You, as an interested party, cannot expect to receive additional compensation and the limitations imposed will effect the use of the land, the value of the land and possibly the ability to transfer the land in the future.

Inverse Condemnation

Another form of condemnation that may occur is inverse condemnation.

Inverse Condemnation is a form of condemnation that occurs when a property owner demands that his land be purchased from him.

Example: An inverse condemnation suit might occur if a property is located at the end of an airport runway.

The noise and pollutants created by the planes might impede the owner's right to quiet enjoyment of his property. This could lead to the property owner demanding that the airport authorities purchase the land.

In some cases, the land itself will not be purchased. If this occurs, the airport may be required to provide the owner with a damage award. These are called consequential damages and such damage awards will only be paid once.

An investor who purchases this land would not be able to collect such an award again but would have a property whose value was diminished by the proximity of the airport.

Example: If a property is located near adjacent to a sewage treatment plant the owner might sue for consequential damages. The property owner might suffer a loss of value due to the odors.

The property owner still has the use of his land but his enjoyment in the land and the value of the land is reduced. The owner would therefore sue for consequential damages.

An inverse condemnation suit that results in the owner retaining the land while receiving a settlement figure for the loss of value would still enable the purchase of the deed or certificate at a tax sale proceeding.

If you purchase a lien certificate or tax deed for a property that has undergone an inverse condemnation suit, you would not typically be able to file an additional suit to compensate you for the reduced value of the land. This would mean that you are purchasing a tax deed to a property whose value has been affected. You cannot expect to gain the loss back through an additional suit.

If you purchase a lien certificate for a property that has suffered an inverse condemnation suit, it is important that you research the potential value of the property. The owner may choose not to redeem such a certificate if the value of the property has been so drastically impacted that there is little purpose to his redemption.

Easement
The government may take only a portion of a parcel of land in an effort to gain access to another area or place specific items upon that portion of the property. This separation of the land is known as an easement.

Easements may also occur privately.

Any real estate investment you make will remain subject to the easement of record until certain actions occur that removes the easement. It is important that you review the section to follow regarding easements so that you may understand the limitations that may be placed upon the land that you purchase and gain the ability to locate the placement and removal of these limitations within the public records system.

PRIVATE LIMITATIONS/ENCUMBRANCES

Private limitations on an estate are typically called encumbrances. The enactment of a private limitation or placing an encumbrance is commonly referred to as removing a stick from the bundle of rights. Examples of encumbrances are private easements, deed restrictions, encroachments, liens, and leases.

EASEMENTS

An easement grants the right to use, or partially use, all or a portion of the land of another individual. The easement does not grant ownership, just the authority to use the portion of the property described in the easement.

Easements may be granted by

- Grant by Deed

- Reservation in Deed

- Contractual Agreement

- Necessity

- Condemnation

- Prescription

Easements may be terminated by

- Release of the easement

- Expiration of the purpose of the easement

- End of prescription or the non-use of another's property.

- Merger of the dominant and servient estates

- End of necessity for the easement

When dealing with easements the estates affected obtain a secondary name.

SERVIENT ESTATE: A servient estate is the land on which the easement exists.

          SKILL BUILDER: The land on which the easement occurs "serves" the other property

DOMINANT ESTATE: The dominant estate is the land that benefits from the easement.

          SKILL BUILDER: The land that receives the easement is the land that dominates the use of the other property.

It is important to the overall value of your investment that you determine any easements that may exist, for or against the property you are considering. The documents listed above will be a part of the public records you will research in preparation for the sale. The following pages will assist you in gaining a better understanding of the types of easements you may encounter and the documents you should review during your preparatory research.

METHODS OF OBTAINING AN EASEMENT

**Deed Restriction/
Reservation in Deed** One method of obtaining an easement is with a deed restriction.

- The easement takes the form of a limitation placed in the deed by the seller.

- Deed restrictions place limits on the buyer and any future owner regarding the use, improvement, or maintenance of the land.

- Deed restrictions are often created to protect those who already have property in the area from a decrease in property values. This decrease could result from the construction of buildings, which are not compatible in value with those owned by the neighboring property owners.

  Example: Scenic views may be impeded by the construction of a high-rise building.

  This may result in a decrease of the value of nearby property.

  A common deed restriction would be to limit new construction height to 15 feet.

  The limitation restricts the buyer or new owner as to how they can use, improve, or maintain the property.

Deed Restriction limitations are enforced though the civil courts. The seller who placed the restriction begins the court action to enforce the restriction. The buyer or future owners are bound by this restriction until it is legally removed through a court action or through another viable method.

- A deed restriction is automatically deemed unenforceable if it requires the law to be broken in the enforcement of the restriction.

- Deed restrictions are usually difficult to remove because all affected parties must agree to remove such a restriction by signing a quitclaim deed.

If you gain an interest in a property that has a specific restriction, you will be bound by this restriction in the same manner as the owners who had an interest in the property when the restriction was placed. It is important that you locate any such restriction and assess the impact this may have on your investment strategy and plans for the property.

Necessity   An easement may also be created by necessity or condemnation.

An easement by necessity is the right or privilege of one party to use the land of another party for a special purpose. This purpose must be consistent with the current general use of the land and be necessary to the party receiving the easement. In case of an easement by necessity, the landowner is not dispossessed of his land; he simply coexists with the holder of the easement.

Common easements by necessity include those given to utility companies to run their lines over private property or the right of people to walk or drive across someone's land to reach another piece of property.

An easement by necessity occurs when the easement is necessary for the use of a person's property or land.

Example: If a seller sells the back portion of his property to a new owner, the back portion may be landlocked unless the buyer is given the right to access the portion.

This access would be obtained by traveling over the front portion whose ownership is retained by the seller.

The seller cannot land lock the new buyer so an easement by necessity is granted.

When purchasing a property at tax sale that is subject to an easement by necessity, you would be required to comply with the terms of the easement when making use of the investment.

Example: In the previous example, we showed an easement by necessity that granted the buyer of the back lot the right to gain access to the lot over the lot retained by the seller.

This right automatically becomes included in the sale if the back lot is sold or otherwise conveyed. The need to comply with the easement will also affect the front lot if it is transferred.

If you purchase either lot during a tax sale process, you will become subject to the same restrictions or benefits created by the easement as the owner who held title to the property when the easement was created.

When you are researching potential investments, any easement that affects the lot you are considering investing in will affect the use and the value of that lot. The effect on the front lot is often termed a burden. Whenever the front lot is sold or conveyed, the new owners must continue to respect the easement to the back lot. If you gained the front lot, you would be required to continue and respect the easement to the back lot. Similarly, if you gain the back lot at the sale, you would have use of the easement provided by the front lot in the same manner as the previous owner.

Example: If you purchase the front lot, you would not be able to erect a fence around the property. The erection of the fence would block the easement access granted to the back lot.

The front lot serves the back lot so it is termed a servient estate. The back lot would become the dominant estate.

The process of providing an easement granting access to the back lot is termed the granting of a right of way. The receipt or granting of any easement or right of way will become apparent to you during your research.

Contractual

A contract may be created that provides a person a specific grant to an easement.

An owner may reserve specific rights or withhold rights of an easement in the wording of the deed granting the property to another party.

Example: A land developer might reserve easements for items such as utility lines or access to additional parcels when selling lots to a purchaser.

Any contract or special document that effects the investment you are considering may affect your use of your new purchase. You should remember that all recorded documents you locate must comply with the statutes and jurisdictional regulations in your area. If you locate such a document and feel that it may limit the use of your planned investment, you may wish to make further inquiry into the legality of the items included. If the inclusions comply with statute and jurisdictional regulations, you will be bound by all stipulations.

Prescription

A method that may create an easement without a written document is called easement by prescription.

Prescription is the term for an easement process where the easement results from the open (observable), continuous (uninterrupted), notorious (public) and hostile (adverse to the owners title without the owners permission) use of the property.

In other words, this occurs when a person constantly uses a perceived easement over a period. If a person behaves in a manner that shows he owns an easement long enough, he will have made the ownership legal.

This method of obtaining the legal right to the property of another individual is termed adverse possession.

Example:

> A neighbor uses a path built across the property you are bidding on to access the State Forest that abuts the property.

>> This use is considered to be open because they simply walked across the property.

>> The use is considered exclusive because it was the only method employed to access the State Forest.

>> The use is considered notorious because the neighbor made no effort to hide their access.

>> The use is considered hostile because the neighbor did not ask permission to use the pathway.

> This taking infringes on the rights of the true and legal owner.

> If the period prescribed by statute ripens into an actual title it is said to be possession commenced in wrong and maintained by right.

> Simply stated, the initial possession of the property was notorious or hostile but the statute allowed the property to become rightfully owned by the new possessor.

> Adverse possession is based on the applicability of the statute of limitations.

> These statutes allow a specified time in which the legal owner may recover the property. If recovery is not completed within this time, the statute allows for the theory that the property has been abandoned to the adverse possessor.

It is important that you review not only the public records that pertain to the investment you are considering but also view the property itself. There are various reasons you will wish to view the property. We will review many of them in a later chapter. For now, you should consider that you might note possession issues that may limit your rights to the property despite your investment. If you do note adverse use of the investment, you should then research the specific statutes in your area to determine the status of the use.

Encroachment Another method of creating an easement is through the process of encroachment. Encroachment is the unauthorized intrusion of one's real property ON, OVER, or UNDER the land of another.

These encroachments may include:

- Tree roots

- Overhangs on Buildings

- Boundary line confusion when building

The property owner suffering the encroachment has the right to force the removal of the encroachment. If the encroachment is not removed within a certain time, it may then become and easement by prescription.

It is important that you gain a comprehensive understanding of land descriptions of every property you are considering as an investment. This ability to locate the boundary lines of the property will assist you in determining possible encroachments that may have occurred. If such an encroachment exists, it will be a crucial portion of your planning to determine if the encroachment has ripened into an easement by prescription or if you, as the new investor owner, will have the ability to remove this encroachment from the property.

Easement in Gross At times, an easement may be granted to a person or business that is not a neighboring property owner. This easement is known as an easement in gross, and in this type of easement, there is no dominant estate.

Example: A utility company is granted the right to run their lines over one's property.

These easements belong to the utility company and are no longer a part of the parcel of land.

All future owners of the land will be bound by the easement in gross.

An easement in gross may also be granted to an individual. These may include the right granted to a friend or neighbor to walk over the land of their neighbor to access a particular private spot.

In this instance, the easement in gross is for personal use and is not a transferable easement. The easement would end with the death of the person holding the easement.

METHODS OF TERMINATING AN EASEMENT

At times, you may encounter an easement that has been terminated. Understanding the methods of termination will assist you in deciding if a specific item you located is, in fact, an issue or if it has been resolved. Easements can be terminated by

- The release or end of the need for the easement

- The expiration of the purpose for the easement

- A merger of the dominant (the land which benefits from the easement) and servient (the land on which the easement exists) estates

- The end of the necessity for the easement

- In case of prescription, the easement may be terminated by the non-use of the property in a manner that is open, continuous, notorious, and hostile

It may be possible for you to put an end to an easement that exists with regard to the property whose deed you obtain. This issue will require further research. For investment purposes, it is always best to assume that an obvious easement will remain part of the title you gain until you have proven otherwise.

CHAPTER

6

ADDITIONAL RIGHTS

At times the property may carry with it additional rights. These additional rights will transfer with the property and an investor obtaining a tax deed or tax lien certificate will gain an interest in these rights. You should consider any additional rights you might gain an interest in when assessing the properties potential value as an investment.

S ome additional rights are necessary for the use of the property. An example of a necessary right would be the right of access. Without access to the property, the use of that property would be very limited. Other rights might enhance the value of a property. A property that contains Riparian rights would provide the owner of the property the right to use a river or stream located either on or at the border of the property. This could enhance the perceived value of the investment.

ACCESS

When examining the property it is important to determine if the property abuts or adjoins another property or a public road or access.

An abutting property is a property where the real estate touches a public road or another piece of real estate.

- If the property abuts a public road, you must determine if direct access to that road has been conveyed or condemned by the government. The conveyance or condemnation of access could be a serious question when making an investment at tax sale. You will not usually have the opportunity to quiz the owner of record with regard to the property. In many cases, the only information you will gain regarding a property before you purchase at the sale is that information you can observe from the border of the property and the vital elements of information you will gain from the public records.

- There are two different types of access.

Physical Access: Physical access is the actual ability to use an access point to the property. In some instances, a property may abut one or more roads but legally lack the right of access or the use of all of the roads.

The abutment to these roads would be physical access but because of the fact that the access points are not legally described to the property, they are not considered physical. In other words, the simple existence of a point of access does not necessarily mean that an owner of the property abutting or adjoining the access gains the right to use it. You must conduct further research to ensure that the property you are considering contains legal access points.

Legal Access: Legal access is the legal right to use a described access point to a property.

In most cases, the location of a legal access point for the property you researching provides you with the ability to gain entry into the property once you have completed the purchase. Legal access is crucial to the potential value and uses of your new investment.

There will be times that a legal access described in the records does not actually provide a simple method of gaining entry to the property.

A property may be described as having the right of access to a road that does not yet exist. This right of way may be planned in the future and legally established and therefore can be contained in the records you are researching. However, since the right of way or access is planned rather than actual, you may not have the rights to gain entry to your property using that access point until some date in the future.

In some instances, you might gain use of this described legal access by actually creating the road or entry described in the document.

This is often a very expensive and time-consuming endeavor and so the potential profit of such a venture must be carefully considered before you invest.

Your investment strategy will often dictate the importance of immediate access to a particular parcel.

    o If you are purchasing a long-term investment with an eye toward increased real estate values for a future sale, existing access today might not be as much of an issue providing there is the hope for eventual legal access.

    o If you are purchasing short-term investment property with the plan of flipping the real estate on the general market for an immediate profit, you will wish to consider the impact a lack of actual access might have on the marketability of your investment.

When researching access there are some additional considerations that should be considered as each may alter the value of your investment.

QUALITY   You must note the quality of the right of access.

This means that the access might be other than vehicular.

Example: Pedestrian – foot traffic only

Aquatic – via water only

Some other non-conventional form of access.

The quality of the access should be confirmed during your search. The quality of the access might affect the value of your investment as well as the potential uses you might put the property to in the future.

BOUNDARY LINE AGREEMENTS

You may encounter items that reference boundary line issues when you are conducting your research. Such issues may also become apparent when you are viewing the property in which you are interested in investing. If there appears to be an issue with the boundary lines of the property, you should review the public records to see if you can locate any reference to an established agreement. Whenever the location of the boundary line division between two properties cannot be accurately determined, the value and potential use of your new investment could be affected

- You should research the records to determine if a boundary line agreement has been created and recorded between the concerned parties. Most States will allow the enforcement of an existing boundary line agreement by tax deed or certificate investors.

  If no such agreement exists, you may still determine that the investment potential outweighs the issues that may arise.

- Following your purchase, you might have an accurate survey conducted at the property to clarify the boundary lines of the property. In order for the survey to be of a benefit to you, you must then create and record a valid boundary line agreement between you, if you have gained an ownership interest and the other concerned parties.

  If you have completed a survey but are unable to negotiate an agreement with the other property owner, you may complete proper judicial pleadings and proceedings to obtain a judgment that clarifies the boundary lines.

- The most common situations that cause boundary line problems are:

  - Gaps

  - Overlaps

  - Imprecise descriptions

  - Improper location of fences

  - Improper location of boundary markers

  - Accreted land

  - Errors in surveys

  - Recorded sub-division maps or land plats

  - Defective legal descriptions

RIPARIAN RIGHT

Another example of an additional right that may be granted with the conveyance of a particular property would be Riparian right. The transfer of ownership of a parcel of land that borders on a river or stream will typically carry with it the right to use that water in common with other landowners whose lands border the same watercourse. This additional right could greatly enhance the potential value of your investment.

When dealing with Riparian right the landowner does not have absolute ownership of the water that flows past his land but may use it in a reasonable manner.

In some states, the riparian rights have been modified by the doctrine of prior appropriation.

- The doctrine of prior appropriation allows that the first owner who is able to divert water for his own use may continue to do so although it is not equitable to the other owners along the watercourse.

LITTORAL RIGHT

Similar to Riparian rights, littoral rights may exist. If a parcel borders a lake or sea, it is said to carry littoral rights. The inclusion of littoral rights with your investment could greatly enhance the potential value of the investment.

- Littoral rights allow the landowner to use and enjoy the water touching his land provided he does not alter the position of the water by artificial means.

Ownership of land typically allows the right to drill for water, which may be found below the surface of that parcel of land.

In some states, a landowner has the right to act in conjunction with the neighboring landowners to draw his share of percolating water.

In other states, water rights are limited by the doctrine of prior appropriation.

- The doctrine of prior appropriation states that the first landowner to divert the water for his use may continue to do so although the diversion of this underground water may not be equitable to all landowners.

ACCRETION

Another factor that may affect the land, which borders an area of water, is accretion.

- Accretion is the process by which a piece of land is increased or extended by the gradual deposit of soil as a result of the action of a river, stream, lake, pond or mass of tidal waters that border the property.

If an accretion exists, the description of the land you are considering might have been altered since its creation. This could provide you with additional land beyond that described within the records you are searching.

When you purchase a parcel of land that has been increased through accretion, you can modify the land description by the obtainment of a land survey of the property that shows the new boundaries. You will want to compare the legal description of the property you are considering with the legal description of the property shown in the tax rolls. This allows you to ascertain if the property to be insured has been properly assessed and that the taxes have been fully paid. If there is an issue concerning legal description and tax assessment, you might become liable for the assessments that should have been applied in the past if you become the owner of record to that property.

FLOOD PLAIN

When you are considering an area of land that borders any body of water, another important item must be researched. You will need to determine the flood plain status of the property you are considering. The designation of flood plain may have created limitations as to the uses you may make of a particular parcel, may influence the perceived value of your investment, and may make the investment virtually unusable.

A parcel of land need not border a body of water to be designated as a flood risk. You should consider the potential designation of any investment you are considering to ensure you do not make a purchase that cannot be used for the purpose you intend.

Flood designations are easily located within the public records you are searching or through the applicable agencies.

BEACH PROPERTIES

If a portion of a property you are considering contains beach area, other factors might affect the value of your investment and the potential uses.

Before investing in beach property, you should conduct further research to determine whether the title to the wet-sand area is constitutionally, statutorily, or judicially considered to be held in trust by the government. If this is the case, the use of the beach property may be designated as public and, in most cases, the beach property will not transfer ownership among private individuals regardless of the sale methods employed.

You should also review all records to determine whether the public may have acquired the right to use any part of the beach area or any part of the upland for the purpose of access to the beach area. Adverse use or local custom may have granted this right to the public. If you obtain ownership interest to the property, the uses you might put the property to may be limited by this custom or adverse use.

Example: If the public has gained the right to use the beach area or the actual property for access to the beach area through custom or adverse use, you might not be able to fence the entire property. This action would be limited because this fencing would limit the use of this access by the public.

STRUCTURES

The chapter regarding the rights and interests in land detailed for you the surface rights, including improvements that might be gained through your investment. It is important that you actually view the property you are considering prior to making any investment or purchase. The improvements to the land may not be adequately described within the records you are researching. Actually viewing the property will allow you to determine many important factors that will affect the value of your investment. One piece of vital information you may gain is the status and type of structures that exist.

You will want to screen your investments with an eye toward future expenses that may be incurred with regard to that investment. To purchase a property at tax sale that has a perceived value of $75,000 with a simple investment of $2,500 may appear at first glance to be an incredible return. However, you might find if you do not assess the improvements before the purchase, that the structures contained upon your new investment require you to expend additional sums to achieve the expected value from that investment.

You will typically not be able to gain access to the interior of the potential investment prior to the sale, but there are many determinations you might make from the curb. These observable items will provide vital clues as to additional expenditures that you will have to make before obtaining full value from your investment.

There have actually been instances where a property purchased at tax sale without adequate review by the investor was actually under an order by the zoning and code enforcement agencies for demolition. To purchase an improved property based on perceived value of that improved property is only a benefit to the investor if the improvements are in a condition that they can be easily used or transferred. You might still invest in a property that requires extensive funds for repair, but must factor these expenses into your strategy. This will enable you to gain a proper understanding of the probable profit you will obtain from the investment.

CHAPTER

7

FORMS OF OWNERSHIP

When researching potential investments in the public records system it is important to understand the forms of ownership you may encounter. Earlier we emphasized how important it is to search every owner who might have caused a claim to be made against the title. In order to verify that you have adequately researched the actions of every owner, you must understand the different types of interest that exist.

R esearching potential encumbrances, liens and other defects established by the primary owner is an effective beginning in determining the potential value of your investment. However, you must always remember the title might be affected by actions of other individuals with an interest in the property. Understanding the forms of ownership can assist you in ensuring that you have researched the actions of all owners. This will elevate the possibility that you have gained all the needed information regarding possible limitations of the property investment you are considering.

Sole Ownership   Sole ownership is also known as Tenancy by Severalty. This means the ownership is cut off from other owners or the individual owns the property alone.

In Sole Ownership, the term individual may refer to a variety of entities. Ownership must be a single entity but can include:

Married or single individuals

Corporations considered a single entity

Specific limitations and rights of ownership interests possible by unusual entities are detailed later in the coursework.

This form of ownership is both created and disposed of by deed or will.

When a sole owner holds the title to the property you are searching, you need only locate the matters pertinent to that owner to determine what matters might effect the value and use of the investment. You should remember that actions of owners who held the property before the current one will also affect the uses and value of the property. You must search backward in time to determine the interest methodology used by each owner and then conduct the appropriate research.

Concurrent Ownership

Ownership may also be concurrent ownership. Concurrent ownership is the ownership of a property by two or more individuals.

These owners can share one of five different unites.

- **Unity of Time**   They may have the Unity of Time, which means that both parties acquired their interest at the same instant in time.

- **Unity of Title**   They may share the Unity of Title, which means that their interest was acquired by the same instrument.

- **Unity of Possession**   They may share the Unity of Possession. This means that each party has the same, undivided right to possess or use the property. In the Unity of Possession, all portions are owned equally.

- **Unity of Interest**   They may share the Unity of Interest. The Unity of Interest means that each owner has an equal interest regardless of the amount they contribute or their desire to have different interests.

- **Unity of Person**   They may share the Unity of Person, which means that each owner owns the property as a unity or team. An example of this would be a married couple forming one legal unit in the process of ownership.

Concurrent ownership may take many forms. These forms are referred to as a type of tenancy.

1. **Tenancy by the Entirety**

   The parties united by the tenancy of the entirety are married individuals.

   This is the only instance in concurrent ownership where the individuals will share all five forms of unity.

   This form may be created by deed or will and may be disposed of only jointly by deed.

   This form of tenancy does contain a right of survivorship. Right of survivorship is the right of the surviving co-owner to acquire the deceased co-owner's share in the property automatically.

   If the parties in tenancy by the entirety are divorced, the tenancy by the entirety automatically terminates and then becomes a tenancy in common.

2. **Joint Tenancy with the right of survivorship**

   Joint tenancy with the right of survivorship is held by two or more individual entities.

   This tenancy shares all forms of unity EXCEPT the unity of person.

   This form of tenancy may be created by deed or by will and may only be disposed of by deed. Each individual may sell their share in the ownership without the consent of the other party.

   This form of tenancy does contain the right of survivorship that means the remaining parties obtain the ownership interest of the deceased member upon his death. The right of survivorship defeats the effect of a will.

3. **Tenancy in Common**

   Two or more individuals in common hold tenancy.

   The only form of unity required to create a tenancy in common is the unity of possession. There may be other unities in existence.

   This form of tenancy may be created through deed, will, or divorce.

This form of ownership may be disposed of through either deed or will without the consent of the other party.

This form of ownership does not contain the right of survivorship so each individual may dispose of their interest at the time of their death as they choose.

It is important that you gain a comprehensive understanding of all of the different interests that may be created and terminated. This will enable you to locate each successive owner within the records you are researching. Any action taken by any interested owner can influence your position with regard to your new investment. The items included with each of the chapters you have completed should be viewed as applying to every owner with an interest in the property. Researching the actions of only one owner or the most obvious owner will not provide you with the security you require before risking your investment dollars at the tax sale.

TAX LIEN AND TAX DEED SALES

CHAPTER

8

LIENS AND ENCUMBRANCES

The most common and perhaps important limitations you
will find when researching a potential investment are those
imposed by liens.

You may be planning to attend a free and clear sale where the taxing authority has taken steps to abolish liens held by others that exist against the property. It is commonly believed that the term free and clear dictates that all existing liens and encumbrances against a property have been removed and that the tax sale investor will obtain full rights of ownership with no liability other than the costs incurred by the winning bid amount. Unfortunately, this is not the case. Regardless of the type of sale you attend, you must conduct research to determine what matters might affect the value and uses of your investment.

Example: State and Federal Liens will not be abolished even with a full foreclosure proceeding by the taxing authority.

Example: Other liens may have been recorded after the date of the judicial foreclosure conducted by the taxing authority.

Any investment in a tax sale property requires attention to the potential limitations, liens and other matters that exist within public records. The notices that the individual conducting the tax sale read at the commencement of the sale will specify these research requirements, but the investor who does not realize the implications of the notices until the start of the sale will not have the tools necessary to successfully profit from tax sale investments.

Regardless of the type of sale, you plan to attend; adequate research into the public records system will enable you to enter the sale and bid, confident that you have a comprehensive understanding of both the benefits and the obligations your new purchase will bring you.
You may be planning to purchase a tax deed or tax certificate at a subject to sale.

- In this type of sale, the tax lien takes priority but the other liens against the property will still exist.

  You should always verify the status of all liens and other encumbrances to ensure the security of your investment.

- If you attend a subject to deed sale, you will become the new owner of record for any property where you place the successful bid. This ownership interest dictates that you are purchasing the interest subject to all existing claims, liens, encumbrances, and other matters.

  These existing items can greatly affect the potential value and use of your new investment.

It is imperative to a successful tax sale venture that you gain all knowledge possible with regard to any matter that exists against the property you are considering. You may still find it profitable to purchase a deed that contains liens and other encumbrances, but will want to research potential value and the status of the repayment of these items more closely.

Example:	You purchase a tax deed for a property worth	$75,000
	The total up-front investment at tax sale is	$ 2,500
	Perceived profit potential	$72,500

This investment shows an incredible opportunity for profit.
However, you must consider any other liens that might exist.

Example:	Expected Value	$75,000
	Sale Investment	$ 2,500
	Existing Water Lien	$ 800
	Recorded Mortgage	$12,000

General Federal Lien	$ 5,100
Perceived Profit Potential	$54,600

An investment with these liens may still provide an excellent opportunity.

- You would have the ability to sell the investment on the general market gaining full value and paying off all other liens.

  This would provide you with up to $54,600 in potential profits against your initial investment of $2,500.

- You might also redeem the other liens against the property investing an additional $17,900 to clear the title and gain full use of the property.

When you are conducting research into a potential investment, you must research the status of any lien that you locate to determine if it can be collected or if it has been abolished through a proper procedure. This will enable you to determine the potential effect each lien will have on your investment.

The first step in understanding how to locate and research potential liens against the property you are considering is to understand the types of liens that may exist.

Liens can be classified in two categories. These are the voluntary and involuntary lien. Within these categories may be two types of liens, specific liens and general liens.

VOLUNTARY LIEN   A voluntary lien is created when a property owner voluntarily creates a lien against the property in order to borrow money.

> Example: A mortgage lien would be an example of a voluntary lien.

INVOLUNTARY LIEN   An involuntary lien is created through the operation or enforcement of the law.

> Example: A property tax lien
>
> A mechanic's lien
>
> A judgment lien

An involuntary lien is often the result of inaction on the part of the debtor or a failure to pay as agreed.

Both types of liens will be recorded within the public records you are searching. Within these two categories are types of liens that must be understood.

GENERAL LIEN   A general lien goes against an individual and attaches to all of the real property of that individual in the county where the lien is recorded.

            Example: Federal and state tax liens are considered general liens.

It is important that you search for any general liens that exist against any owner of record to the property you are searching.

A general tax lien that is recorded against an owner may affect your investment property and may be an item that you must pay in order to retain the rights you purchase in the property.

To locate any general liens that exist in the chain of title, you will search the records by the names of all of the parties who have held ownership interest.

We have detailed the types of ownership interest that can be created to assist you in determining the names of possible owners.

You should conduct a search on each of these owners to assist you in locating any general liens that may effect your investment.

If a general lien exists against any owner of the property, you must conduct additional research to determine the status of these liens. If the liens still exist at the time of the tax sale, you may become responsible for clearing them from the title in order to make use of your investment.

JUDGMENT LIEN   A judgment lien is a lien on all of the debtor's property within the county or jurisdiction of the court issuing the judgment.
A judgment is defined as the final determination by a court of respective rights and claims of parties to an action or suit. The judgment becomes final depending on one of two factors:

1. The expiration of the time to appeal the judgment

2. Lack of a pending appeal

There are many types of judgments. The basic types are:

Declaratory Judgment: A declaratory judgment declares the rights, duties, or status of the parties and/or expresses the opinion of the court on a question of law without ordering any action.

Money Judgment: A money judgment orders the payment of money from one party to another

Federal Judgment: A Federal Judgment is a judgment rendered in a federal court.

Foreign Judgment: A foreign judgment is a judgment rendered by the court of a state or county different from the state or county where the judgment was brought.

Judgment in Rem: A judgment in rem is a judgment on the status or condition of a particular matter and may not require any action.

Judgment in Personam: A judgment in Personam is a judgment against a person not a judgment against a thing or right.

Dormant Judgment: A dormant judgment is a judgment that has not been satisfied but has been in abeyance so long the execution cannot be issued without reviving the judgment. Another term is Expire Judgment.

•   A judgment lien may only be brought by statue.

•   A judgment lien may be brought against the property.

- A judgment lien results from lawsuits for which monetary damages are awarded.

Usually a judgment lien covers only the property in the county where the judgment is recorded but the creditor can extend the lien to property in other counties by filing a notice of lien in each of those counties.

The creditor awarded a judgment by the courts can request the courts issue a writ of execution. This writ allows the county sheriff to seize the property and sell a sufficient amount to pay the debt and the expenses of the sale.

If any judgment exists in the records with regard to the property you are considering, the status of the judgment should also be researched.

A subject to sale and many certificate sales will allow the judgments entered into record to remain against the title to the property.

This means that the judgments must be paid upon the liquidation of that property.

Some free and clear deed sales will allow specific judgments to remain after the judicial foreclosure process.

Regardless of the type of sale you attend, you must conduct research into the public records to determine what judgments exist, the status of those judgments and the potential obligations you will incur with the investment into a property against which these judgments are secured.

TERMINATION

Judgment liens may terminate in a variety of methods. If you locate a judgment lien with regard to the property investment you are considering, you should research to determine if the judgment has been terminated.

The primary methods of termination are:

1. Lapse of time – expiration

2. Full payment and subsequent satisfaction of the judgment

3.   Release of the real property from the lien by the creditor for whom the judgment was generated.

4.   A merger occurs in which the creditor for whom the judgment was created becomes an interested owner in the property against which the judgment was executed.

5.   Sale of the judgment

6.   Vacation of the judgment

7.   Reversal of the judgment in a court of appeal

8.   The title of the property against which the judgment is placed is lost to adverse possession.

9.   Provisions set forth by local statutes.

Other possible remedies resulting in termination are possible but these are the most common

SPECIFIC LIEN

A specific lien goes against a specifically identified property.

Example: A property tax lien is a specific lien because it is a lien against a specific piece of property and no other.

Mortgagees and mechanics liens are also specific liens.

These liens apply only to the noted property and therefore the failure to pay these liens cannot result in the forced sale of other property held by the debtor.

It is important to your search to determine what property a particular lien is held against and the effect these liens do or do not have on the property you are researching.

LIEN ENFORCEMENT

If the enforcement of a lien becomes necessary, the creditor must ask the courts to sell the property in order to obtain the repayment of the debt. This action is commonly known as foreclosure.

If foreclosure takes place and there is more than one lien holder or creditor attached to the property being sold, the proceeds from the sale are paid according to the priority of the liens.

Gaining interest in a property that subsequently enters foreclosure does not mean that you will lose your investment.

You will have the ability to enter a pleading for your investment, costs, and possibly additional interest. Your abilities at a foreclosure proceeding will be designated by Statute and by the specific Jurisdiction in which you have invested. If a foreclosure action is to be implemented against a property that you are considering as an investment, you will want to review the quantity of liens against the property. You should compare these to the perceived value of the property and the Statutes that will regulate the costs you can claim before making the investment.

LIEN PRIORITY

The priority of the liens is determined by time. The first in time to file or record a lien receives the higher level of priority.

Lien priority can also be determined by specific wording within the recorded documents notifying the public of the lien. This wording is often termed subordination clause and will dictate the status of the lien with regard to priority.

There are some exceptions to the priority by time and specific subordination clauses.

Example: A tax lien would be an example of a lien that would usurp the priority of time.

TAX LIEN

Tax liens are always paid first in order of priority. Tax liens may result from the right of the government to collect real estate property taxes.

- Each tax year, a tax lien is placed on the taxable property.

- This lien is removed when the property taxes are paid.

- If the taxes are not paid, the lien gives the government the right to force the sale of the property in an effort to recover their interest.

When a property is sold at tax sale, a special deed or a specific certificate is issued. The type of sale will dictate what manner of title or certificate is provided to the tax investor.

Ministerial Sales: A ministerial sale occurs when the time specified by statute as the maximum limitation for the payment of property taxes has elapsed. The taxing authority will advertise the sale of a property in the form of notice to the public regarding the intended sale. The conditions and terms of sales of this type are established by the local regulations.

When a ministerial sale occurs, the purchaser acquires a lien against the property for the taxes, fees, and interest owing on the property.

- This lien may eventually result in a title to the property.

- This title is obtained through judicial foreclosure. This foreclosure occurs following a period known as a redemption opportunity. This period of redemption offers the owner against whom the taxes were assessed the opportunity to pay all past due sums, costs and interest penalties assessed. If the title is not redeemed in this manner, the judicial foreclosure proceeding will commence.

Judicial Sale: Judicial sales are conducted under judicial proceedings in which the foreclosure of the property is conducted in an effort to collect the unpaid taxes.

Judicial sales are made following an order or decree of a court of jurisdiction by an officer legally empowered and commissioned by the court. The court then confirms this order or decree.

- In a judicial sale, the court acts as the grantor or vendor in the transaction.

- The officer who conducts the sale is the ministerial agent. Judicial sales can occur for reasons other than unpaid taxes.

MECHANICS' LIEN

The mechanic's lien law gives anyone that has furnished labor or materials for the improvement of a parcel of land the right to place a lien against the improvements and the land. At times, a mechanic's lien may usurp the priority of time. This lien may be placed when the owner of record does not pay services or materials used to improve the property.

To be entitled to a mechanic's lien, the work or materials must have been provided under a contract with the property owner or a legal representative of the owner.

Examples: Mechanics liens that may apply are water liens, utilities, and contractor services.

The theory behind the mechanic's lien is that the labor and materials supplied to the property enhance the value of that property. Consequently, the enhanced property should be used as security for payment. If the property owner does not pay as agreed, the lien can be enforced with a court supervised foreclosure sale.

TERMINATION:

When you locate a lien recorded against the property you are considering as an investment, you must conduct additional research to determine the status of the lien.

The lien may have been terminated through a valid action and such a termination act would appear within the records. Locating termination instruments within the records will enable you to remove the lien from your listing of potential issues that must be remedied to clear your investment.

1.   Payment or satisfaction

2.   Release of the property

3.   Assignment of the lien

4.   Agreement between the parties

5.   Statutory requirements

6.   Expiration of the lien as determined by statutory regulation

7.   Judicial discharge

8.   Statutory bond

9.   Dismissal of the suit

Other possible remedies resulting in termination are possible but these are the most common termination methods you will find when you are conducting your research.

MORTGAGE LIEN   The last form of lien that you will commonly encounter during a property search is the mortgage lien. A mortgage lien is created when the owner of property offers it to a lender as security against the repayment of a debt.

If the debt secured by the mortgage is not paid, the creditor can foreclose on the security property. Following foreclosure, the property is sold to repay the amount owed plus any allowable interest, penalties and other items.

If the foreclosure sale does not provide a sufficient amount of money to repay the debt, some states will allow the creditor holding the mortgage to petition the court to award a judgment of the balance still due.

You should search the public records for all mortgage notices. Upon locating a mortgage notice, you should conduct further research to determine if the mortgage was satisfied or if funds are still owed against the mortgage. Any funds that remain unpaid may attach to the real property that you are purchasing.

FORECLOSURE

A foreclosure proceeding is a legal procedure where the mortgagor obtains the real estate secured by a debt in default for obtaining the funds owed.

- The lien holder petitions the court for the right to sell the property to redeem the monies owed

- The courts and/or the lien holder notify any other individuals who hold interest or liens against the property of the foreclosure proceeding.

This notice enables other lien holders to petition the courts for inclusion in the foreclosure process so that they may gain funds for any funds owed to them that are secured against the property.

- The court issues an order for the sale of the asset secured against the debt

- The real estate is sold to satisfy the debt

- The payment of liens at a foreclosure process occurs based upon the priority of the lien. The first in priority will be paid first from the funds received. Those liens holding later priority will only be paid if the funds received at the foreclosure proceeding exceed those required to satisfy higher priority debt.

- The specific provisions vary by state and you should familiarize yourself with the laws within the state where you will be conducting searches.

If notices indicating that a foreclosure exists in the chain of title you are researching, it is important that you conduct adequate research into the status of the foreclosure proceeding before determining if the property will be a suitable investment for your portfolio.

CONDUCTING THE SEARCH

*The chapters leading to this one have been preparing you
for entrance into the public records room to conduct a
search into the property's you are considering. Now that
you have gained the background you will need, it is time to
gain a better understanding of the layout of the public
records system. This understanding will assist you in
implementing what you have learned to conduct the
valuable research that will protect your investment
dollars.*

Until the enactment of the statute frauds in England and 1677, determination regarding ownership of a parcel of land was usually a matter of simply observing who was in physical possession of the land. A landowner would provide notice to the world that he claimed ownership of a parcel of land by visibly occupying his land.

After 1677, Britain required recorded deeds to show transfers of ownership. Today, both research of the records and visible observance of the land are needed to ensure you have gained as much knowledge as possible regarding your potential investment.

Two methods might be employed to give notice of a claim or right to land.

- One is the recorded document in the public records system to give notice to that effect.

- The other is by visibly occupying or otherwise making use of the land.

The law holds interested parties responsible for examining the public records system and looking at the land for this notice of prior claim.

Constructive Notice Constructive notice is also sometimes referred to as legal notice.

Constructive notice is accomplished by the recording of a document at the county recorder office. Recording the notice:

- Provides notice to the public of the documents existence and contents.

- Charges the public with the responsibility of looking into the public records and at the property itself to obtain all the knowledge necessary concerning who claims interest in a piece of land.

Constructive notice may also be accomplished by visibly occupying the property.

Inquiry notice A person interested in a property is responsible for making inquiry beyond the public records to determine if anyone is giving visible notice to interest in the land.

When dealing with inquiry notice, the law presumes a reasonably diligent person will obtain information by making further inquiry into the ownership of the property.

Actual Notice Actual notice is the knowledge that one has actually gained based on what is:

➢ Seen

➢ Heard

➢ Read

➢ Observed

➢ Witnessed

- If you read a deed stating transfer occurred from Smith to Jones, you have obtained actual notice of the deed and that Smith's claim to the property has been transferred to Jones.

- If you go to the property and see someone has possession of the property, you have actual notice that the people claiming to be there are present.

Remember that anyone claiming an interest or right to the use of a piece of land is expected to make it known by either recorded claim or visible use of the property.

Anyone acquiring an interest in the property is expected to look at the public records system to determine if anyone is making a claim against property and to make visual inspection to determine if anyone is making claim to the property through use.

A critical element to successful tax sale investment is the ability to scrutinize the public records and determine what claims are held against the land.

- The job of tax sale investing is not limited only to attending the sale and placing the winning bid. Perhaps the most essential element of a successful tax sale investor is the ability to protect the investment funds placed at the sale. The bulk of this course is dedicated to provide the tools and knowledge you will require to fulfill this portion of your investment duties.

- Anyone who has knowledge of the date and time of a sale and meets the minimum investor requirements of the taxing authority can attend a tax sale and place a bid. The unschooled individual may be lucky in their choices and make a wise investment at the tax sale; however, the essential factor to building a successful tax sale-investment strategy is to learn to be an intelligent investor, not just a lucky investor.

It is vital that investors have a through knowledge of the public records system and recording practices of the area in which they plan to invest. All states have recording acts that govern the processes of the recording of documents pertaining to the transfer of real estate. These documents are typically placed on file at the Recorder of Deeds office in the county courthouse that governs the region in which the property is located.

Some of the documents, which you may review during a search of the public records system, include:

Mortgages	Notes	Long Term Leases
Options	Deeds	Land Contracts
Easements	Additional Liens	Plot Plans
Mechanics Liens	Releases	

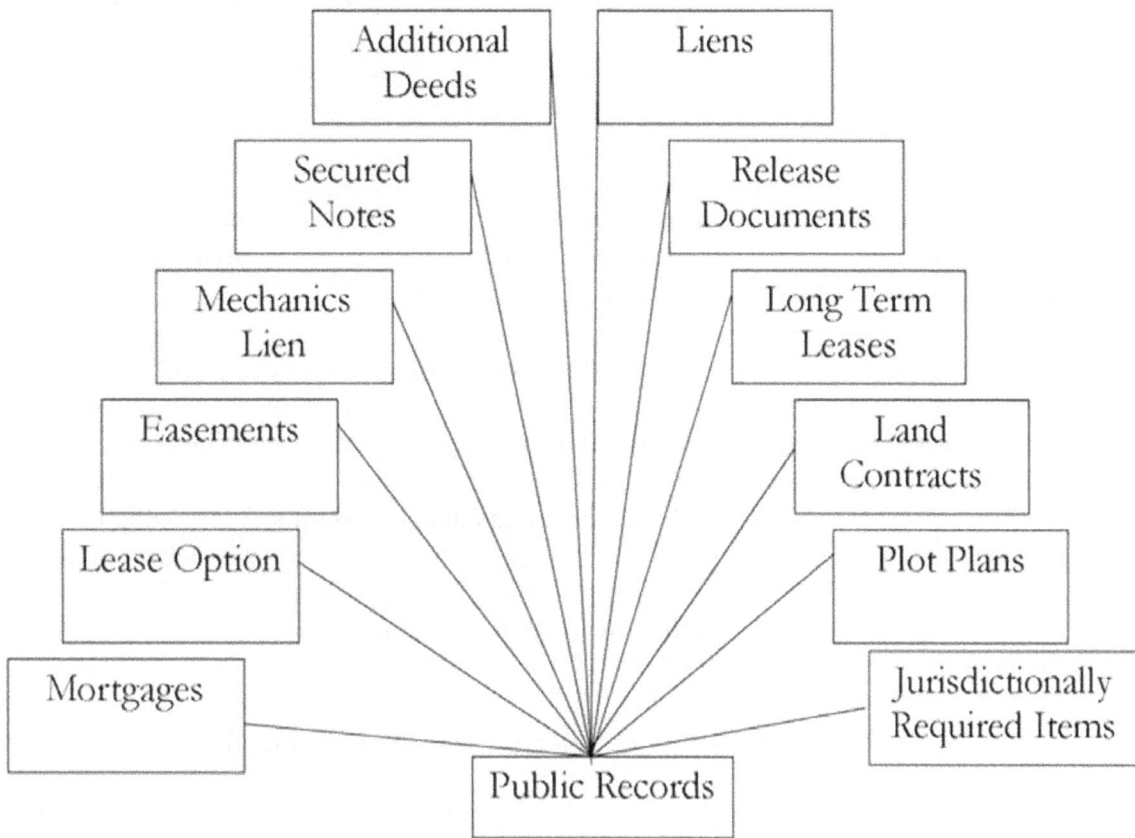

Figure 9:1 – Diagram – Public Records System

The documents recorded within the public records system are done so in a chronological order. This time-based order enables the chain of title to be sufficiently researched backward through time. Each document within the records system will contain a stamp indicating the date and time of recording and be designated by a book location and page number.

- The documents presented for recording will be photocopied and the copies will be placed in the book with indexes.

    The book and index placement will be noted on the document.

    The indexes may take a variety of forms that will be discussed later in this chapter.

- The original copy of the recorded instrument will be returned to the owner for their records.

A through examination of these records allows you to determine what actions previous owners may have taken and how these actions might effect your investment. The results of this examination are also termed determining the quality of the title. In other words, it will show you the condition of the title during the current ownership as well as under previous owners.

All States have recording acts that provide guidelines for the recording of every instrument or document. This recordation notifies all interested parties of any interest or right in land that has been created, transferred, or encumbered.

- Within each state, each county has an office known at the county recorder's office. These can also be termed the public recorder's office, county clerk's office, circuit court clerk's office, county registrar's office, or bureau of conveyances.

- The person in charge of these offices is called the recorder, clerk, or registrar.

- These offices are frequently located within the county governmental offices.

- Each public recorder's office records all documents that are submitted pertaining to real property in that particular county.

- Anyone seeking information regarding ownership of land in a particular county would go to that recorder's office.

- Some cities also maintain a record room where documents are recorded.

- Recording acts permit the recording of any estate, rights, claim, or interest in land.

- Lesser rights are often not recorded because of the costs and effort involved.

  Rental agreements and leases for a year or less fall into this category of leasor rights.

    Many sales require that you fulfill any leaser right previously negotiated for the property you are purchasing while others allow you to negate previously negotiated agreements by providing proper notice to the individuals named.

    You may gain knowledge regarding possible rental agreements and other matters that may effect your investment through the actual inspection of the property.

    Frequent onsite inspection will also reveal the existence of any developing adverse possession or prescriptive easement claim. These are factors often not found by the investor during a search.

- Each document brought to the public recorder's office for recordation is photocopied and returned to the original owner.

- The photocopies are placed in chronological order with the copies of other documents.

- These are stamped with consecutive page numbers and bound into a book.

- These books are then placed in chronological order and shelved in a location open to the public for inspection.

    Binding documents in chronological order is necessary to establish the chronological priority of documents.

DOCUMENT INDEXES

The act of binding documents in chronological order does assist in establishing the priority of all matters affecting a parcel of land, however it does not provide for an easy method of research relative to the land. Indexes have been created to assist the searcher in determining what records exist ore locating each record applicable to a specific parcel of land or the owner of record.

The most commonly used indexes are the grantor and the grantee indexes. Some states use tract indexes.

TRACT INDEX   The tract index is the simplest to use when one is attempting to locate all records applicable to a specific parcel of land.

The tract index allocates one page to listing all of the recorded items pertaining to a single parcel of land.

- The page will provide a listing of all recorded deeds mortgages and other documents that relate to that parcel.

- A few words describing each document will be provided.

- The book and page number where a photocopy of the document will be entered.

If you are investing and conducting research in a State that uses this type of index, you will find your work is greatly reduced. These indexes make researching documents pertaining to a particular parcel an easier process. You must remember though, that actions taken by owners and not designated to a specific parcel may also affect the property you are considering. A search beyond those items listed in this index and into owner-specific records may be needed.

GRANTOR INDEX/
GRANTEE INDEX

Grantor and grantee indexes are alphabetical indexes created yearly and bound in book form.

The basic principal of the Grantee and Grantor Indexes used are the same though the actual appearance of the indexes may vary by jurisdiction.

A grantor index lists all grantors named in documents recorded during a specified year in alphabetical order.

- The grantors are named

- The grantee is named

- The book and page where the photocopied document can be found is listed

- A few words describing the document is entered

The grantee contains the same essential information as the grantor index but the arrangement of the entries is by grantee name.

To use the grantee or grantor index to search public records, you would locate the record for the property owner whose rights are being abolished through the tax sale process.

You would then refer to the specified documents listed under the name of that owner.

- Each of these documents will provide you with information pertinent to your investment.

- You will also use these documents to locate the name of the owner from whom the delinquent taxpayer took title.

You will then repeat the processes for each owner listed on any document pertinent to the parcel you are researching.

The process will continue backward through time until you have located all matters pertinent to the investment.

This process of moving backward and noting every grantor and grantee listed within the document assists you to create a chain of title.

- You should view the chain of title as a group of links moving backward through time.

- If a link is missing from the chain, the connection from the present day to the original grant of the land is not complete.

  The indexes are meant to provide you with the necessary directions to complete this chain.

  If an item exists that breaks the chain, you may need to refer to other indexes, records or areas to mend the break in the chain.

You will use the chain created through your research to assist you in determining any actions that an owner of the property you are considering may have taken to encumber the land. It is important to remember that you must research every owner listed in relationship to the parcel so that you can locate any activity that might affect the value or use of your investment.

There are clues to the depth of research that will be necessary within the documents you review. Specific deeds will provide specific assurance of the status of the title when the deed was created. These deeds may also contain warranties and covenants that will show you the status of the title before the date of the deed. By gaining an understanding of the implications of each deed and the impact the deed may have on your investment, you may limit the work investment required during the research portion of your new investment strategy. The chapter following this one will provide you with an insight into the potential deeds you might encounter during your search, the inclusions of these deeds and the implications of the different deeds that might exist.

PENDING LAWSUITS AND JUDGMENTS

In addition to the other matters you will research, you should make inquiry to determine if there are any pending lawsuits or judgments affecting the title you are searching.

LIS PENDENS INDEX

Most public records contain an additional index known as the Lis Pendens Index. This index will detail pending and unresolved lawsuits within the county that the recorders office serves. You will be interested in any lawsuit that might affect the title or ownership of the property.

You will search the records referenced in this index for any action that relates to any owner of the property you are considering as an investment.

Example: A divorce of a married couple who owned the property is shown within the Lis Pendens index.

The divorce decree issued following the proceedings dictates that only one individual shall hold title to the property in the future.

You must search all records applicable to that property prior to the issuance of the divorce decree that relate to both property owners but may search records following the divorce decree that apply to the partner granted the ownership through the decree.

JUDGMENTS

**GENERAL
EXECUTION
DOCKET**

The General Execution Docket can also provide vital insight into the possible items that might make proving marketable title an issue. This docket shows a detail of judgments entered against an individual.

If an individual who is listed as having ownership interest in the property title you are researching has a judgment entered within the general execution docket, you must note the specifics and conduct further research to determine if a satisfactory resolution has been made of if the judgment might affect the ownership interest of the property title you are researching.

Specifics pertaining to the types of judgments that may exist and the methods of application and termination you should locate for each judgment are included in the previous chapters. You should gain a comprehensive understanding of the methodology for handling judgments so that you can adequately research the records applicable to the property you are considering as an investment.

CHAPTER

10

DEEDS

When you are researching potential investments at the courthouse, deeds will be the most common document you will encounter. The deeds that you will review will come in a variety of formats and types. Each deed will carry different warranties, covenants and restrictions that will affect the investment you plan to make. Gaining a comprehensive knowledge of the format, inclusions and ramifications of each deed is essential to completing the research that will assist in securing your investment.

I t is important to the success of your research that you understand the variety of deeds you will encounter. You must gain a knowledge base that enables you to review the deed to determine its purpose and effect, the forms of ownership that may be conveyed or relinquished by each deed and the warranties, covenants and restrictions that may be placed through the wording of the deed.

To this point, we have emphasized how important a complete search into the public records is to your investment success. This is always true and the most solid investment opportunity is the one that has been properly researched. However, there may be times that the assurances provided by previous owners at the time that they transferred the property you are considering will assist you in minimizing these necessary research requirements.

Deeds
convey or transfer the ownership interest in land from one person or entity to another. Conveyance may be either voluntary or involuntary.

A deed of conveyance
is defined as a written instrument that is executed and delivered by an owner of real property for transferring title or interest in the property to another individual or entity.

The types of transfer deeds you encounter during your research will assist you in determining if further research into the past will be necessary.

Example: If you discover that the owner whose interest in the property you are gaining

- held interest in the property solely

- gained the ownership interest through a fully insured, general warranty deed

- was required to comply with no restrictions as to the use or actions of the land

- retained the full bundle of rights to the property

You may only find it necessary to research the documents pertaining to the present owner's term of ownership.

Example: On the reverse, if you discover that the owner whose interest in the property you are gaining

- obtained their interest through a quit claim deed

- was subject to numerous land use restrictions

- segregated the mineral rights to the property with the intention of selling these rights to another party

You will wish to research the chain of title to determine the status of the many defects that are apparent. You will wish to determine:

- whether the owner in question actually held full interest in the property

- whether the ownership held was sole ownership or if it was shared with another individual

- that no obligations still exist from previous owners

- what land use restrictions still exist with regard to the use of the property

- that the sale is for the property rather than the mineral rights

The following explanations of the deeds you may encounter, the warranties, and covenants they may include and the implications of each will assist you in determining the depth of research you must conduct on each potential investment.

GENERAL WARRANTY DEED

A general warranty deed is considered the highest form of deed that a buyer can receive from a seller and is the deed that you will encounter with the most frequency during your search.

The general warranty deed states that the Grantor (seller) warrants good, clear title to the grantee (buyer) and agrees to protect the grantee from any defect in the title whether the defect occurred during the seller's ownership or that of previous owners.

> The essential component that makes this type of deed the most desirable to obtain is the warranty that title is a good, clear title throughout history and places the responsibility for defending any defects that may exist on the shoulders of the seller.

> The use of this type of deed will allow you to feel a higher level of certainty that the title prior to the creation of this deed was reasonably researched and considered a good title.

This implies that you should only research those matters that may have occurred after the date of this deed. You will wish to make your own determination based on any other documents discovered within the records you are searching, but this is a solid baseline rule you can integrate into your investment strategy.

GRANT DEED

A seller using the grant deed for conveyance provides warranty of a good, clear title only during his term of ownership and does not warrant the condition of the title prior to his possession of the property.

> In a general warranty deed, the grantor makes himself responsible for the encumbrances of prior owners as well as his own actions.

The grant deed limits the grantor's responsibility to the period of time he actually owned the property.

The grant deed is similar in nature to the special warranty deed and will sometimes fall under the same terminology.

The location of a grant deed may imply that it is prudent to research all actions pertaining to the property you are considering that may have occurred both before and after the creation of this type of deed.

The mere existence of this type of deed does not guarantee that an issue exists, but it should be considered that the grantor creating this deed had knowledge of an issue that occurred prior to his ownership that he did not want to take responsibility for correcting. A wise investing decision is to locate this issue and determine its potential impact on your investment.

SPECIAL WARRANTY DEED

The special warranty deed is similar in nature to the grant deed. When conveying a property using the special warranty deed, the seller warrants the property title only against defect occurring during the seller's ownership and not against any defect existing before that time.

Executors and trustees who speak on behalf of the estate often use the special warranty deed. The executor or trustee has no authority to warrant or defend the acts of previous owners of the title.

In some states, the special warranty is known as the bargain and sale deed.

In summary, the grantor warrants good, clear title to the grantee and agrees to protect and defend the grantee from all defects in the title that occurred during the grantor's ownership. In other words, the seller is guaranteeing that he has cleared the title from all defects during his ownership but is making no guarantees as to the condition of the title because of the actions of previous owners.

The ramifications of locating this type of deed in the records of the property you are considering are similar to those of the grant deed.

BARGAIN AND SALE DEED

The basic bargain sale deed contains no covenants and only the minimal essentials of the deed. The deed

- Identifies the buyer and the seller

- Recites consideration

- Describes the property

- Contains words of conveyance

- Contains the seller signature

The deed has no specific covenants incorporated into the wording. When conveying a property using the bargain and sale deed, the seller only implies that he owns the property described in the deed and makes no guarantees as to the condition of the title or even his or her ownership interest.

> The grantor implies that he owns an interest in the property but conveys the property without any warranty to the grantee.

In this case, it would be most prudent to complete a full research action into the public records surrounding the property you are considering. It is within the title of a property that contains a deed of this type that most unexpected issues will arise.

QUITCLAIM DEED

A quitclaim deed has no covenants or warranties whatsoever.

The grantor using this type of deed is making no warranties nor are they even implying that they own the property.

Whatever right the seller possesses at the time the deed is delivered is conveyed to the buyer.

- If the seller has no interest or title to the property described in the deed no interest is conveyed to the buyer.

- If the seller possesses fee simple title, the fee simple title will be conveyed to the buyer.

The critical wording in a quitclaim deed is the seller's statement that he does remise, relief and quitclaim forever.

- Quitclaim actually means to renounce all possession or interest.

- Remise means to give up any existing claim.

If the grantor of a quitclaim deed subsequently acquires any other interest in the property, he is not required to convey it to the buyer.

Initially this type of deed may appear to have no effective use. However, situations often arise in transactions when a person will claim to have a partial ownership interest in a parcel of land.

Such an ownership interest is often discovered as a title defect or cloud of the title. These may result from an inheritance, community property, or mortgage foreclosure sale as well as from other means.

- The individual, who releases any claim to the fee simple title by enacting a quitclaim deed, would remove a cloud on the fee owner's title.

- The quitclaim deed can be used to create or provide relief from easements.

- The quitclaim deed can be used to release remainder and reversion interest.

- The quitclaim deed can be used to remove the interest of a party in a creative financing scenario.

When enacting a quitclaim deed, the Grantor coveys whatever interests or claims they have in a property without any warranty or the implication that they own a portion of the property.

The quitclaim deed is often used to clear an exiting blemish on a title and it is important to review the wording of the deed to determine the reasons the quitclaim deed was used.

In some cases, the use of a quitclaim deed may prove beneficial to your investment by removing an interest that might have otherwise created an issue with your investment.

In other instances, the use of a quitclaim deed may create additional questions regarding your investment that you should attempt to answer through further research into the records.

GIFT DEED

A gift deed is created when the phrase for money or other valuable consideration is replaced with the statement in consideration of his or her natural love and affection.

This phrase may be used in a general warranty, special warranty, or grant deed however; it is most often used in a quitclaim or bargain sale deed.

The location of a gift deed does not necessarily affect the method of search you may choose to conduct. However, the type of deed used in conjunction with the gift deed and the warranties and covenants included may assist you in determining additional or fewer research criteria that you should implement.

GUARDIAN'S DEED

A guardian's deed is used to convey a minor's interest in a property. This deed must contain the information that the legal authority usually, the court order, permits the guardians to convey a minors property.

**SHERRIFF DEED/
REFEREE DEED**

The Sheriff or Referee deeds are issued to a buyer when a person's real estate is sold because of a mortgage or other court ordered foreclosure sale.

This type of deed conveys only the foreclosed party's title and carries only one covenant.

> This covenant states that the sheriff or referee has not damaged the property title.

It is important that you review the title carefully when this type of deed exists. This type of deed frequently leaves unresolved issues in existence because a property owner whose property is taken by this type of action frequently has other matters against them that may affect the title to any real property they own.

**DEED IN LIEU OF
FORECLOSURE**

A deed in lieu of foreclosure may be created in an effort to avoid the full foreclosure action. The debtor conveys to the lender the property, including any equity, in consideration of the removal of all obligations to pay an agreed upon debt.

A deed in lieu of foreclosure may only be executed after the default on the part of the debtor.

It is important that you review the title carefully when this type of deed exists in the chain of title. Transfer using this type of deed frequently allows unresolved issues to remain in existence that may affect the title to the property you are searching.

CORRECTION DEED

A correction deed or deed of confirmation is used to correct an error in a previously executed and delivered deed. These can be used if an error was found in the spelling of the names or property description.

A quitclaim deed is often used to the same purpose.

A correction deed may also be called a deed of confirmation or a reformation deed. The accepted uses for this type of deed are extremely limited. This type of deed may only be used if item to be corrected is

- Clerical or Typographical

- A result of a lack of clarifying information

- To cure a defective acknowledgement

The location of a correction deed should be noted in that any alteration to any item included in your research listing might be cause for you to begin the search process again using the corrected information.

CESSION DEED

A cession deed is a form of quitclaim deed where a property owner conveys certain rights to the county or municipality.

When a cession deed is located, it is important that you note the owners whose interest is being transferred. Any other individuals who held interest at the time the cession deed was created will retain their interest after the cession deed.

The cession deed removes the interest of the individual providing conveyance through the deed into the future. Any actions that the owner took with regard to the property that pre-date the session deed must still be researched as they may still affect the title.

INTER SPOUSAL DEED   An inter spousal deed is used in some states to transfer real property between spouses.

The location of this type of deed may remove one owner of research from your listing because from the date of the deed creation forward, this owner will no longer be able to incur obligations against the property. It is important to remember that while you may cease researching for actions that occurred after the recording of this deed in relationship to the non-owner spouse, actions may still exist prior to the recording of the deed that might affect your investment.

TAX DEED   A tax deed is used to convey title to real estate that has been sold by the government when the owner of record fails to pay the taxes assessed against the property.

The deeds you encounter vary greatly in nature, format and inclusions. It is critical that you gain the knowledge you will need to review each deed applicable to your potential investment and determine what rights or restrictions are incorporated into the document. The deeds detailed in this chapter include the most common deeds ones that you will encounter during your research. You may locate other forms of deeds but each will carry essential components that enable it to be considered a legally binding document. The following pages will provide you an example of the basic components of a deed. The deeds you review will also carry specific disclaimers or warranties that assist in protecting the parties to the transaction. Each entry on the deed should be reviewed so that you may become familiar with the forms you will encounter as well as the items of restriction or warranty that you should note. These restrictions and warranties may affect your investment.

- The wording of the deed will outline components that protect both parties in the transaction, restrict actions or grant rights.

- A deed must contain some components to qualify as a recordable document under the guidelines of the recording requirements of the jurisdiction where the transfer occurs.

Parcel ID No.

File No.

JUDIICAL SALE IN CONNECTION WITH THE TAX SALE OF 20___

DEED

OF

TAX CLAIM BUREAU OF ANY COUNTY, ANYWHERE

Made the _____ day of _____, Two Thousand _____ (20___)

Between the TAX CLAIM BUREAU OF _____ COUNTY (the latter a subdivision of the City of _____ with a seat of government in the Borough of _____ County of _____ and Commonwealth of _____) as constituted and created by virtue of the provisions of the Act of Assembly approved the 7th day of July, 1947, P.L. 1368 (72 PS 5860.101) and known as the "Real Estate Tax Sale Law" as supplemented and amended, as trustee for

Owner or reputed owners, herein designated as Grantor of Party of the First Part;

AND

of the City of _____, County of _____, and Commonwealth or State of _____, herein designated as Grantee or Party of the Second Part;

Witnesseth THAT WHEREAS, the real estate hereinafter identified was exposed to the Tax Sale duly held by the First Party on the _____ day of _____, 20 ___, as continued, adjourned, or readjourned, under and by virtue of the provisions of the Act of Assembly hereinbefore identified and the upset price was not bid by anyone is such Sale; and

WITNESSETH, THAT WHEREAS, by proceedings filed to No. _____ a Decree of the Court of Common Please of _____ County, was entered directing that said property be sold at a subsequent date fixed by the Court, free and clear of all tax and municipal claims, mortgages, liens, charges, and estates, of whatsoever kind, with the purchaser at said sale to have an absolute title to said property, free and clear of the claims aforesaid;

AND WHEREAS, the Second Party became the purchaser, (or is the heir or assignee of said purchaser) of said real estate at the Judicial Sale held by the First Party on the _____ day of _____ A.D. 20 ___, as continued, adjourned, or readjourned, under and by virtue of the provisions of the Act of Assembly hereinbefore identified.

Figure 10:1 – Sample Tax Deed – Page 1

NOW, THEREFORE, WITNESSETH, that under and in pursuance of the Act of Assembly aforesaid and the Order of Court entered in connection, therewith, and for and in consideration of $_____ _____ Dollars, in hand paid, the receipt of which is herewith acknowledged, (being the price bid at said Judicial Sale), the receipt of which is herewith acknowledged, (being the price bid at said Judicial Sale), the Grantor or Party of the First Part, under and by virtue of the Act of Assembly aforesaid as Trustee for the owner or reputed owner of said Real Estate, does hereby grant, bargain, sell, assign, and release, in fee simple, unto the said Grantee or Party of the Second Part, their heirs, successors, and assigns,

ALL

Control # 060-0027

Map # 0800-21-17B

For chain of title see DBV 1128 page 116

All taxes up to and including 20____ County and Township were in sale.

Realty transfer tax is $_____ for 1% Local and $_____ for 1% State, based on the Common Level Ratio Factor at the time of the sale, which was 11.91%.

TO the end that said purchaser shall take and hold an absolute title to the said property free and clear of all tax and municipal claims, mortgages, liens, charges, and estates of whatsoever kind, except ground rent separately taxed.

TO HAVE AND TO HOLD the said premises, without warranty of any kind or nature, unto the said Party of the Second Part, their heirs, successors, and assigns forever.

IN WITNESS WHEREOF, the said Party of the First Part set its hand and seal the day and year aforesaid.

TAX CLAIM BUREAU OF

By _____

Figure 10:2 – Sample Tax Deed – Page 2

This form is included for example purposes only. The form is modified from the acceptable real estate forms as released by HUD. The services of a real estate professional should be retained to ensure the correct forms are used for your transaction.

TAX CERTIFICATE
SEC. 197 FS

Tax Deed File #

Property Identification #:

    The following Tax Sale Certificate Numbered 37496 issued on 2004 was filed in the office of the Tax Collector of this County and application made for the issuance of a tax deed, the applicant having paid or redeemed all other taxes or tax sale certificates on the land described as required by law to be paid or redeemed, and the costs and expenses of this sale and due notice of sale having been published as required by law, and no person entitled to do so having appeared to redeem said land; such land was on the 27th day of April, offered for sale as required by law of

being the highest bidder and having paid the sum of his bid as required by the Laws of

NOW, this 27th day of April,   the County of   , State of   , in consideration of the sum of $16,957.00 being the amount paid pursuant to the Laws of   does hereby sell the following lands situated in the County and State and described as follows:

Beginning at the westerly line of Abbot Ave and
CR 401 thence as described DB 1922 Pg 49

_____(SEAL)
                     Clerk of Circuit Court

Figure 10:3 – Sample Tax Certificate

This form is included for example purposes only. The form is modified from the acceptable real estate forms as released by HUD. The services of a real estate professional should be retained to ensure the correct forms are used for your transaction.

The following pages provide a sample of a deed parts with which you will wish to become familiar.

FORM   The deed must take the form required by statutory law if any exists.

NAMES   The names of the parties, both the buyers and the sellers, must be included on the deed.

> Marital status and name changes should be included in this portion of the deed.

> Name changes can be noted as "formerly known as..."

CAPACITY   The parties to the deed must have legal capacity to enter a binding agreement as defined by statute.

CONSIDERATION   A statement that the property is being sold for payment must be included.

> This is the purchase price of the property.

> In some states, you may maintain the privacy of the transfer by inserting a nominal amount of money plus other consideration a phrase such as "$1.00 plus other good and valuable consideration".

> Consideration may also take the form of a gift.

GRANTING CLAUSE   The granting clause states what act the parties are performing with the endorsement of the document. In other words, this clause signifies the intent of the seller to convey his or her interest in the property to the buyer.

LEGAL DESCRIPTION   The legal description is a very exact description of the property that will enable one to locate and identify the property to be conveyed and distinguishes the property from all other real estate.

RECITAL   The recital identifies previous owners from whom the current grantor took title.

> The recital will aid you in gaining information that will assist you in researching the chain of title.

TAX LIEN AND TAX DEED SALES

REALTY TAX STAMPS Tax stamps are added to the document at the courthouse at the time of recordation. These stamps provide proof of the payment of the state and local taxes due when transferring real estate have been paid.

TO HAVE AND TO HOLD CLAUSE Also known as the Habendum, the have and to hold clause is the technical language that describes the ownership interest in the property that is being transferred through the enactment of the deed.

GRANTOR'S SIGNATURE The grantors (sellers) must sign the deed.

The grantee (buyer) does not need to sign the deed)

ACKNOWLEDGEMENT Acknowledgement is best known as notarizing. This is the event where the sellers appear before a notary or other approved person to prove and declare that the signing of the deed and the transfer of the deed is a voluntary act.

CERTIFICATE OF GRANTEE'S ADDRESS The certificate of address is a requirement that must be incorporated into the deed document in order to record the deed. It provides the information applicable to the new owners such as full name and address and enables the taxing authorities to send all future notices and tax bills to the grantee.

RECORDING REFERENCE The recording reference is added by the clerk off record and it specifies the date, deeds book volume, and deed-book page number where the recorded document is filed.

DELIVERY AND ACCEPTANCE While there is no requirement that the grantees sign the deed document, the last legal step in the transfer of the deed is the delivery and acceptance of the conveyance. The grantee must receive and accept the document. This acceptance finalizes the transaction and conveyance of the property has been achieved.

Delivery may be actual or constructive.

ACTUAL DELIVERY is the physical transfer of the deed before the death of the grantor.

CONSTRUCTIVE
DELIVERY

is the delivery in cases where the law implies the existence of delivery by the conduct of the parties involved.

WARRANTIES OF TITLE

A deed that meets of all the legal requirements of recordation could leave some questions unanswered.

- The grantor will include certain covenants and warranties in the deed.

- Specific covenants and warranties that are written promises by the grantors regarding the condition of the title may be included in the deed.

- The grantor may also guarantees that if the title is not as stated he or she will compensate the grantee for a loss suffered.

Five different covenants have evolved over the centuries for use in deeds. The inclusion of any of these covenants could provide additional assurance to you with regard to the condition of the title at the time the deed was created.

The deeds you review may contain none, some, or all of these covenants and warranties. Additional warranties may exist within the jurisdiction in which you conduct your search. It is an essential portion of the job of the investor to obtain a full understanding of these guarantees. These guarantees, like the specific deed types named earlier in this chapter, will assist you in determining what additional items of research you may need.

COVENANT OF SEIZIN   under the covenant of Seizin, the grantor guarantees that he is the owner and possessor of the property being conveyed and that the seller actually has the right to convey the property.

COVENANT OF ENJOYMENT   Under the covenant of enjoyment, the sellers warranty or guarantee that the buyer will not be disturbed by someone else who might claim an interest in the property.

**COVENANT AGAINST
ENCUMBRANCES**

The covenants against encumbrances is when the seller guarantees to the buyer that the title is not encumbered with any easements, restrictions, unpaid property taxes, assessments, mortgages, judgments, etc. except as stated in the deed. If the buyer discovers an undisclosed encumbrance, he can sue the seller for the cost of removing it.

COVENANT OF FURTHER ASSURANCE

The covenant of further assurance requires the seller to procure and deliver to the buyer any subsequent documents that might be necessary to make good the buyer's title.

WARRANTY DEED FOREVER

Warranty deed forever is the guarantee to the buyer that the seller will bear the expense of defending the buyer's title. If at any time in future, someone else attempts to and is able to prove that he is the rightful owner of the property, the seller will bear the burden of the costs incurred. The buyer can sue the seller for damages up to the value the property.

Because the warranties that might be included within a deed could prove costly if an issue becomes apparent in the future, the seller sellers often back them up with title insurance.

COVENANT OF RIGHT TO CONVEY

The covenant of the right to convey is an assurance that the grantor has the right to convey the property to the grantee. In some jurisdictions, this warranty is covered under the covenant of seizin.

COVENANT OF NON-CLAIM

The convent of non-claim assures the grantee that neither the grantor nor his heirs or assigns will claim any title to the property being conveyed.

Before you invest in any property, you should to confirm that the needed covenant or warranty is included. If the covenant or warranty that provides the needed comfort level for your investment strategy does not exist, you must conduct the additional research recommended within this coursework.

LIMITATIONS IN THE DEED

At times, the deed may contain limitations regarding the rights and interests being transferred to the buyer or the actions the buyer may take in the future regarding the piece of property. These limitations can vary depending on the specific situation and the needs of the parties. These limitations typically affect not only the buyer named in the deed that contains the limitation, but all future owners. You will be affected by the limitations imposed just as any other buyer of the parcel named. In general, limitations take one of three forms.

EXCEPTION   Exceptions withhold or exclude a part of the estate being conveyed from transfer through the transaction and represent specific property rights that are not being granted to the buyer.

> Example: A common exception would be if the grantor required the use of an easement across a portion of his property being sold or conveyed to access another portion of his property that is being retained.

RESERVATION   Reservations are clauses that reserve an interest in the title being conveyed. Reservations are created in the favor of the grantor.

> Example: A common reservation would when the seller wishes to retain the mineral rights of the property.

RESTRICTIONS   Restrictions may be incorporated into the deed as a limitation on the future action a buyer may take with the property.

> Example: A common restriction would be to limit new construction on the property to buildings of less than 15 feet in height. This restriction would protect the scenic views of other property owners in the area.

Each entry on the deed and the specific wording, inclusions and type of deed within the public records of the property you are considering as an investment will provide information that assists you in determining the value of the property to your portfolio.

CHAPTER 11

Property Location and Descriptions

After you have conducted courthouse research into the properties on the list that are of interest to you, you should then visually inspect the property. A visual inspection can provide you with as much information regarding your potential investment as the courthouse research you conduct.

P hysically locating and viewing the property you are considering adding to your investment portfolio is as important to your success as the research that you conduct within the courthouse records.

- You must be certain that the property you are purchasing is actually located where you expect it to be.

  Many undereducated real estate investors have left the tax sale excited by the purchases they made only to discover that the parcel or property they purchased is not where they expected.

- You must determine exactly what it is you are purchasing.

  Viewing the land will enable you to determine what, if any, improvements exist and the condition of these improvements.

- You must gain a comprehensive understanding of the descriptions you will encounter during your research so that you know how to locate the property boundary, determine the shape, and confirm that the property size conforms to the description within the courthouse records.

  All of the physical aspects of the property will affect the value of your purchase.

We have discussed locating property in the tax assessor's map and we have discussed reviewing property descriptions to determine the exact location, boundaries, and possible limitations regarding the property and its use. Now you must use those same maps and descriptions to locate the property so you may perform the best physical inspection possible.

- The property you are inspecting may or may not be vacant.

- The property may or may not be accessible for viewing.

Due to the nature of the purchase you are planning to make, the physical inspection you conduct will often need to be a visual inspection completed from outside the boundaries of the property. If the property is unoccupied, it may be a simple matter to conduct the external inspection on the property. If the property is occupied by the delinquent taxpayer, they will typically not wish to have you on the property to assess its potential.

Regardless of the ability you have to access the property, you can still gain valuable information from an exterior visual inspection. This information may assist you in determining the strength of the property's investment potential.

- The ability to access the property from a public or private roadway will become apparent when you locate the property. Access is critical to the ability to use and or develop the property.

- The upkeep of any structures that exist, including roofing, siding, other structural issues will provide you with multiple forms of data that might affect your investment.

  Noting items that will soon need to be repaired replaced or are currently in poor condition will provide you with information regarding additional expenses you may incur if you obtain the deed to the property.

  This inspection will also provide you with information regarding the probability of the property retaining value until the redemption period expires.

  Example: If the roof is faulty, additional damage may occur during the redemption period that will lower the value of your investment.

Noting the current owner's maintenance of the property may provide you with clues as to the present owner's interest in his property.

Example: A property that appears neglected may indicate that the property owner will have little interest in paying the certificate costs. This may result in you acquiring a deed to the property rather than a cash return on your investment.

- Determining the occupancy status could assist you in creating a strategy pertaining to the use of the property. Depending on the type of investment you are investigating, the occupancy status of the property can dramatically affect your potential for gain.

  Example: If you are seeking a deed property that appears vacant, the lack of occupancy may indicate to you that no one will redeem the property before the sale. This supposition allows you to rank this property as a higher status on your probable purchase list.

  Example: If you are seeking a certificate property, an unoccupied property may indicate that the owners have determined they no longer desire an interest in the property. This possibility may lower the status of the property on your desirability list. An owner who has determined he will give up his property and vacated will not likely make payment to you. This minimizes your cash return potential until the redemption period has expired and you can take possession of the actual deed and property.

- Physically viewing the property will enable you to determine the existence or lack of improvements.

  If the property is improved, the value may be increased and the possible uses you could make with the property upon acquiring the deed will be enhanced.

  On the other hand, if the property contains improvements that are close to or within the condemnation range of condition you may be responsible for the removal of the improvements upon acquiring your investment.

- The first rule of real estate investment is location, location, and location.

  The location of a property can have a dramatic impact on the property value and the potential uses for that property.

  The neighborhood in which the property is located including potential value reducing uses will be critical to the overall value of the investment.

The zoning of the property will affect the uses you may put your investment to after the sale and may influence its value.

Included in the section under location should be the availability of utilities. Many investors purchase land at tax sale. It is important to be certain that the necessary utilities for the use you plan are available.

> Physically seeing the land does not guarantee the needed utilities, will be available but can provide vital clues in making this determination. In addition, if you contact the authority that provides the utility, they may request information from you regarding the exact location of the property. You can only provide these details if you have actually seen the property.

- Viewing the property, even without the ability to gain entry, enables you to assume certain things about the property features.

    Example: The visual inspection may show a chimney indicating to you that the property likely has a fireplace.

    The addition of a fireplace may increase the property resale value should you acquire the deed.

    Example: On the other hand, the visual inspection may show you that the property has an old coal flue and no other apparent updates.

    The fact that the property is heated by coal and apparently has no updated source of heat may dramatically decrease the value of the property. Any issues such as these may require you to invest additional funds to update the heating system if you acquire the deed.

- External factors or environmental factors may affect the value of your investment.

    Whether acquiring a tax lien certificate or a tax deed your primary goal is the retention of value in the property until you have received your return.

    Example: If you visually inspect the property, can clearly see that the property sits in a flood zone, and has a high probability of flooding on a regular basis you may feel that the investment could depreciate.

The items included on this list are examples of opinion regarding potential knowledge you might gain from a visual inspection of the property. These items should not be considered an all-inclusive list. The reasons provided for the inspection of these items are illustrative examples and should not be considered legal advice or a final decision indicator.

The following pages will provide you with insight into the different types of property description and location references that you may encounter during your research.

LAND LOCATION

Many times, property is easily located by street names and numbers. Sometimes, the property you are considering may not be so easily identified.

- The property may be located in a rural setting that makes it difficult to pinpoint its exact location.

- The map number might be the only method of identification used to describe the property on the tax sale lists.

- The property address might be similar in name to multiple locations making the determination of which parcel is being sold difficult.

Numerous other location issues might exist that make having knowledge of the format of the records within the courthouse critical to your ability to locate the parcel.

Land is described using a variety of methodology. Each method refers to the same parcel. The ability to review various methods of reference and confirm the location of the property you are considering as an investment using each method is essential to the success of your investment strategy.

1.   **INFORMAL REFERENCE**

Informal reference is the description of land by the street numbers and place names.

Example: 123 Realty Street

The advantage of the informal reference method is that it is easily understood.

The disadvantage of the informal reference method of describing land that it is not a precise location that is easily confirmed as the parcel you are attempting to locate. Street names and numbers describing a parcel are often similar to those describing another parcel and can be confused. The informal reference does not provide exact boundaries of the land and the numbers and names of the streets used in informal reference tend to change over the years making it an unreliable descriptive method.

It is often best to reference more than one descriptive method to ensure that you have correctly identified the property being offered at the tax sale.

2.   METES AND BOUNDS

The second method of land description is the metes and bounds method. The metes and bounds description is a more exact method of describing the location, form and boundary of real estate.

Monument	The metes and bounds description method uses a permanent, man-made monument or reliable fixed location as a beginning point for the description.

This monument is set at one corner of the parcel and is typically an iron pin or pipe that is driven several feet into the ground. At times, a concrete or stone monument is used. To guard against the possibility that the monument might later be removed, it is referenced by means of a connection line to a nearby permanent reference mark established by a government survey agency. |

Reference Mark	Other parcels near the one being described will also be referenced to the same permanent reference mark.

This permanent reference mark allows for easy re-structure of the beginning point for the metes and bounds measurements regardless of the passage of time or the alteration of the post or pin location.

You will see the metes and bounds method of description in many older deeds you encounter during your research. It is important that you learn to construct a specific drawing based on the description so that you can locate understand the exact boundaries of the property you are considering. |

Distance and Direction	After affixing the post or pin to a corner of the property, the surveyor then describes the parcel in terms of distance and direction from that point.

The metes and bounds method actually translates as

- distance (metes) and direction (bounds)

- The direction + the distance = the side

The distances in the description are usually expressed in feet but any linear measurement may be used for descriptive purposes. Other linear measurements that may be seen are yards, miles, perches, and rods.

- Direction is shown in degrees, minutes, and seconds |

> ➤ 360 degrees in a circle
> ➤ 60 minutes in each degree
> ➤ 60 seconds in each minute

- To obtain the directions to include in the components you would determine the primary direction to be used.

  The primary direction is either north or south.

- Next, you take the degrees of deviation from the primary direction.

  The degree of deviation will not exceed 90 degrees.

  The degree of deviation will deviate from the primary direction toward one of the two secondary directions.

- The secondary directions are east and west.

With the metes and bounds system you would start from the permanent reference mark and use the direction and distance to travel to the nearest corner of the property.

- This is the point where the parcel survey begins and it is known as the point of beginning or point of commencement.

- From this point, you would travel clockwise along the parcel perimeter. Although it is possible to describe a parcel by either going clockwise or counter clockwise, it is customary to go clockwise.

At times, the survey will be so old or the land so changed that it is difficult to locate the survey pin on the actual property. Using the permanent monument as a starting point and then following the directional measurements to locate the corner of the property will assist you in gaining the knowledge you need to locate the boundary of the property, any encroachment issues that may exist and to confirm which improvements are erected on the property you are considering as an investment.

Diagramming Quick list:

1. Locate the Point of Beginning

2. Identify the Direction from the Point of Beginning

3. Identify the Distance to the next point

4. Repeat the steps until you have outlined 4 sides

Example: Begin at the point on the Western side of 1st Avenue and at the intersection of lots 3 & 4 of the plot plan.

Continue along the northerly side of lot 3 SOUTH 60 degrees WEST 120 feet to an alley.

Along the EASTERN side of the ally proceed NORTH 59 degrees WEST 60 feet.

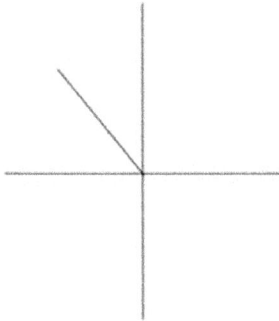

Thence continue NORTH 60 degrees EAST 120 feet thence along the same line.

Continue SOUTH 58 degrees EAST 59.6 feet to the place of beginning.

Diagramming Directions

1. North 45 Degrees West   2.   South 15 Degrees East

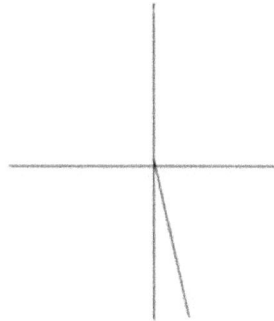

Figure 2:1 Diagramming Directions

3.   RECTANGULAR SURVEY

Another method of land description is the rectangular survey system. This method is sometimes alternately termed a government survey or US public land survey.

The rectangular survey system is designed to provide faster and simpler methods of describing land than the metes and bounds method. Rather than using available physical monuments, the rectangular survey system is based upon imaginary lines.

- These lines are the east-west latitude lines and the north-south longitude lines that encircle the globe.

In terms of landmass, more land in the United States is described using this rectangular survey method than by any other method. If you are reviewing the actual number of property or parcels documented the recorded plat is used more frequently.

It is important that you learn to

- Understand how to read this type of description.

- Compare the recorded description against the property you are searching.

- Be able to locate the property on the plot maps from the description in the event it becomes a necessary part of your investment research.

Principal Meridians	Principal Meridians is the first item to understand in the rectangular survey method. Certain longitude lines are selected as principal meridians and it is upon these lines that the remaining lines are calculated.
Base Line	For each principal meridian there is an intercepting latitude line called a base line.
Correctional Lines	Every 24 miles north and south of a base line are correction lines or standard parallels.
Guidelines	Every 24 miles east and west of the principal meridian, guidelines are placed to run from one standard parallel to the next.

These are needed because the earth is a sphere. As one travels north or south, the longitude lines come closer together until they eventually meet at the farthermost north and south points of the globe.

Each set of standard parallels and guide meridians outline a section, which contains 24 mile by 24-mile area. These areas outlined are called a check or quadrangle.

2nd Standard Parallel North

	1st Standard Parallel North	
	Base Line	Check
	1st Standard Parallel South	

Figure 11:2 – Sample Diagram – Rectangular Survey 1

- Selected Longitude and Latitude lines serve as Base Lines and Meridians

There are 36 principal meridians and the intersecting base lines in the US public land survey system.

Every six miles east and west of a principal meridian, imaginary lines are drawn.

This creates 6-mile wide columns, which are then called ranges. These ranges are numbered consecutively east and west of the meridian.

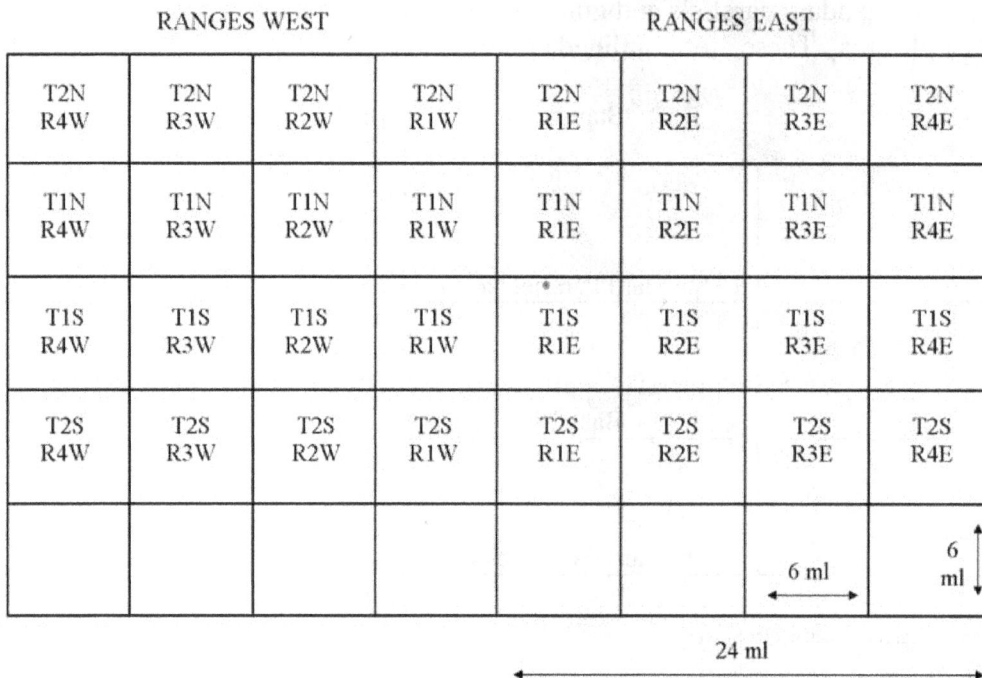

RANGES WEST   RANGES EAST

T2N R4W	T2N R3W	T2N R2W	T2N R1W	T2N R1E	T2N R2E	T2N R3E	T2N R4E
T1N R4W	T1N R3W	T1N R2W	T1N R1W	T1N R1E	T1N R2E	T1N R3E	T1N R4E
T1S R4W	T1S R3W	T1S R2W	T1S R1W	T1S R1E	T1S R2E	T1S R3E	T1S R4E
T2S R4W	T2S R3W	T2S R2W	T2S R1W	T2S R1E	T2S R2E	T2S R3E	T2S R4E
						6 ml	6 ml

24 ml

In turn, every six miles north and south of the base lines another line is drawn. These lines are known as township lines.

These township lines are then numbered in a similar manner to the ranges with the numbers increasing as you move away from the line.

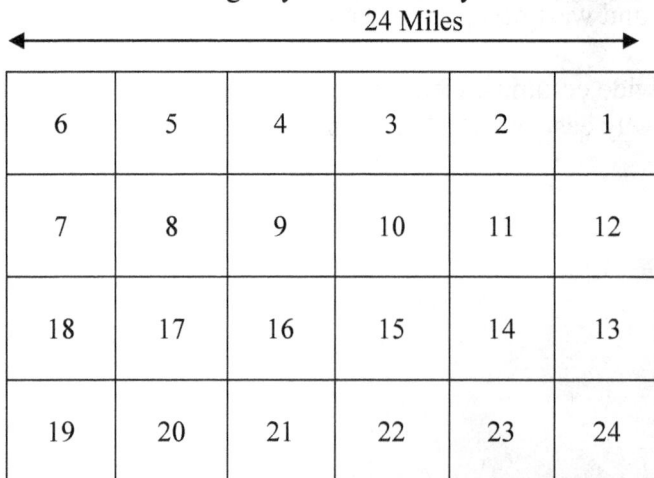

24 Miles

6	5	4	3	2	1
7	8	9	10	11	12
18	17	16	15	14	13
19	20	21	22	23	24

Figure 11:4 – Sample Diagram – Rectangular Survey 3

Each of these imaginary boxes created by the ranges and township lines measures 36 square miles. These imaginary boxes are commonly called townships.

Each of these townships is divided into a 1 square mile portion termed a section. Sections are numbered 1 to 36 beginning in the upper right hand corner of the township and continuing left to right until the sections have all been numbered. In this method, any sections numbered consecutively share a common boundary.

Each 1 square mile section contains 640 acres.

Each acre contains 43,650 square feet. Any parcel of land smaller than a 640-acre section is identified by its position within the section. To do this each section is divided into quarters and halves. This division allows parcels, which are smaller than 640 acres to be identified.

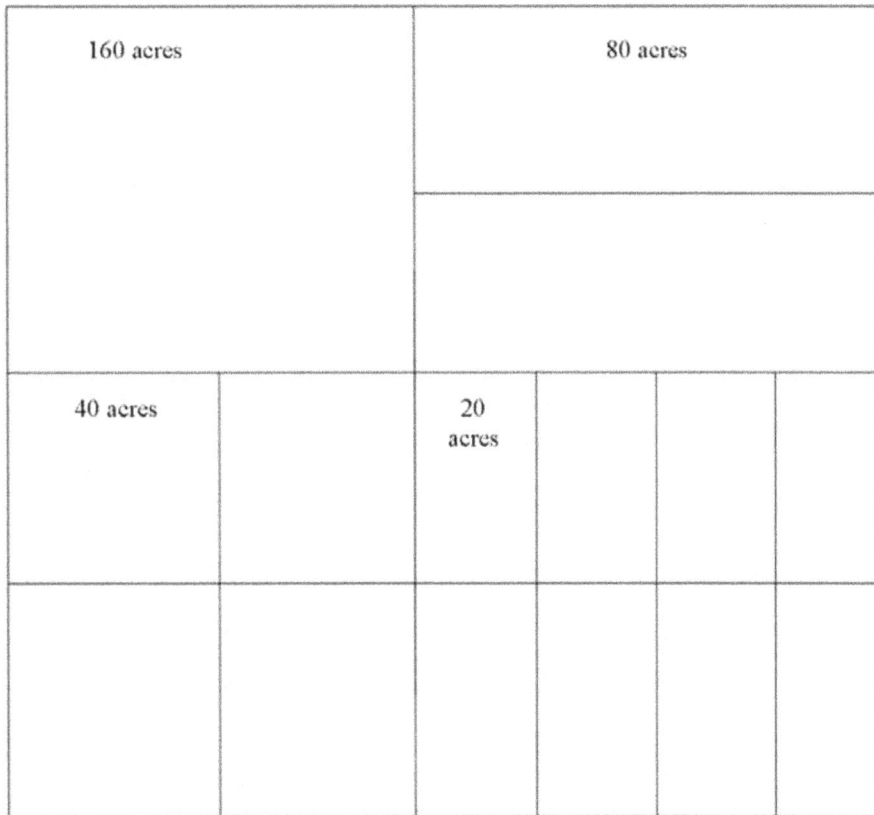

Figure 11:5 – Rectangular Survey

Dividing a section into a quarter creates 160 acres.

Dividing quarter section by quarters creates 40-acre parcels and so on.

If you are attempting to locate or sketch a rectangular survey, it may be helpful to start at the end or smallest section in the description and work your way outwards.

Some sections using this method will be smaller than the 640 acres. This is because the longitude lines of the earth converge as they near the North Pole. For this reason, not all townships will contain 36 square miles.

4.   **RECORDED PLAT**

Another method of land description is the Recorded Plat method. This is the simplest and most convenient method of describing land.

- A plat is a map that shows the location and boundaries of individual properties.

- This system is also termed the lot-block-tract system, recorded map, or recorded survey.

This method is used to describe more parcels of land than any other method. In terms of actual landmass, the Rectangular Survey system is used more often but this system is used for more parcels so you should familiarize yourself with the maps and their form.

This method is based on the filing of a surveyor's plat in the public recorder's office. You will encounter this method frequently when you are reviewing courthouse record maps to obtain an exact property location.

- A metes and bounds survey is typically included in the map and then the map is prepared to show the detail boundaries of each parcel.

- Each parcel is then assigned a lot number.

- Each block in the tract will be assigned a block number.

- The tract itself is given a name or number.

These maps are typically placed in a map book or survey book in the county recorder's office. Each plat is assigned a book and page reference number and all of the books are made available to the public in the county recorder's office.

This system is extremely easy to use once you understand the methods of storage.

- Each area that falls under the county jurisdiction will be assigned to a specific book.

- Most map record rooms contain a legend indicating which book you should search for which area of the county.

- Once you have located the correct book, you will open the maps to the correct page as indicated by the parcel map number you are seeking.

- On that page will be each parcel for that particular area. The parcels will be numbered for easy designation.

You will be able to locate the parcel of land you desire by following the series of numbers provided in the description of the property you are researching.

Plat Map with Assessor's Parcel Number

Example 2: 0200-27-19	0200-27-18	Example 1: 0200-27-17	*Example: Lot 1* *Assessor Log=* *0200-27-17* *Map Book= 200* *Map Page= 27* *Parcel = 17* *Assessor Log=* *0200-27-19*
0200-27-20	0200-27-21	0200-27-17A	*Map Book= 200* *Map Page= 27* *Parcel = 17*

Figure 11:5 – Sample Diagram – Recorded Plat

The first series of numbers included in the description indicates the map book you should select.

Map Page= 27

The second grouping of numbers shows the page of the map book you must reference.

Parcel   =   17

The last group of numbers indicates the actual parcel you would be purchasing. These numbers are typically assigned in a contiguous manner but may sometimes become complex. This complexity is a result of the continued growth in your area.

Example: A map number of 17-1A would be located in the same manner as is detailed in the previous example.

5. ASSESSOR'S PARCEL NUMBER

You may also find reference to the property you are searching in terms of the assessor's parcel number. These are numbers assigned by the tax assessor to aid in the assessment of property for tax collection purposes. Often, the assessor's parcel number and the recorded plat number will be the same in designation.

These parcel numbers are public information and are often used by real estate agents and brokers, appraisers and investors to assist in identifying real property.

The assessor may use a variety of methods to assign these parcel numbers but a common method is to divide the county into map books.

Each of these books is assigned a number. Each book will cover a particular portion of the assessor's county.

Each page of the map book shows specific parcel maps.

Each of these parcel maps will be assigned its own number.

For subdivided lots, these maps will base the numbers on the plats submitted by the sub-divider to the county recorder office when the subdivision was created.

In the case of un-subdivided land, the assessor's office will create its own maps.

Regardless of the source of the maps, the assessor will assign each parcel of land a parcel number.

The assessor's parcel number may or may not be the same as the lot number assigned by the surveyor.

The assessor uses these numbers to produce an assessment roll that lists every parcel in the county assessor's office by parcel number.

> These rolls show the current owner's name, address and the assessed value of the land and buildings of that particular property.

These maps are available to the public in the assessor's office. In some instances, a private firm may reproduce the maps and lists and make them available for a fee.

It is important to understand that these maps are not the final authority for the legal description of the property. The legal description of a parcel can only come from a search that includes looking at the current deed to the property and the recorded copy of the sub-divider's plat.

You will often be able to locate the actual property using these maps. When the property you are considering is not subject to any form of issue, this basic location may be sufficient. If an apparent issue such as encroachment exists, then you will want to research further into the records to obtain exact metes and bound style or other exact description to assist you in establishing boundary lines.

6. REFERRAL TO ANOTHER DOCUMENT

Land is also sometimes described by referring to another publicly recorded document.

Example: A deed or mortgage may be referenced to aid in describing a parcel of land.

> All that certain lot, parcel, or piece of land described in Deed Book Volume 109, Page 67 at the County of Records.

To be used as reference these documents must contain a full description of the parcel in question. If you encounter a document that only contains a description that references another document, you will need to access this other document in order to obtain the information you require.

7. STATE REFERRAL METHOD

Some states have developed their own, statewide system of reference points for land description and surveying.

Example: In North Carolina, the state is divided into a grid of 84 blocks.

Each side of these blocks corresponds to 30 minutes (1/2 of 1 degree) of latitude or longitude.

This method is called the Grid System and these grid lines intersect at points to which the metes and bounds system can be referenced.

These systems may also be termed coordinate systems and are frequently put into place to help with the surveying of large parcels of land in remote areas.

It is important that you establish the methods of land description used in your State or Jurisdiction. A local or regional investor will probably not need to understand all of the methods of land description described in this chapter. It is important that you familiarize yourself with the methods you will encounter. This allows you to obtain all of the needed knowledge to feel secure that you are making the correct investment decision.

8. SURVEY

A survey is defined as the process of measuring land to determine its exact area.

Surveyors report a map or plat in the form a drawing that shows the exact

- Measurements

- Boundaries

- Areas

- Improvements

- Structures

- Easements

- Utilities

- Features

of a certain parcel of land

Survey requirements are established by each individual state. There are minimum survey standards established by the American Land Title Association and the American Congress of Surveying and Mapping. These standards may be added to or modified by the State in which the survey is conducted.

To be considered valid, a Licensed or Registered Land Surveyor or a Licensed Civil Engineer must complete a survey. State Law may authorize other individuals to conduct surveys within that particular State. If a question arises as to the competence and authority of a specific surveyor, it is best to research the authorization through applicable state agencies before using the survey provided.

Reviewing surveys for the purpose of tax sale investment requires a fine attention to detail. Some of the items you will wish to consider are:

- The land record system that was used to develop the survey

- The compliance of the survey and surveyor with the State and General Survey licensure requirements

- The access to and from the property described in the survey

- Whether the legal description included in the survey and on the title and deed match

- Whether the legal description of the property to be purchased matches those descriptions of neighboring properties with no conflict

- Whether those matters affecting the property such as easements, utilities and other items shown on the survey create potential use issues for you after the purchase

APPURTENANCE

In addition to the basic description of the property, the conveyance of land carries with it any appurtenances to the land. An appurtenance is any right, privilege, or improvement that belongs and passes with the land but is not necessarily part of the land.

Example: A common appurtenance would be an easement or right-of-way that was gained for that particular parcel of land.

Restrictions and appurtenances will be explained more fully in a different section of the course. These items are being mentioned here because you will often encounter notations regarding these matters during your review of land descriptions.

When reviewing legal descriptions various items may appear and affect your investment's potential. Any item that you find in the legal description may require additional research to ensure the investment you are considering will provide the value you are seeking and can be used in the manner you wish.

CHAPTER

12

QUICK LISTS

PREPARATION QUICK LIST

1.   Obtain listing of property scheduled for sale

2.   Review the public records to determine status of the title

3.   Confirm any outside assessments that might exist outside of public records including water, sewer, trash, city code liens

4.   Compare property to similar property listed for sale in the MLS whose location is close to the property you are considering. You may also determine the sale prices of similar property sold within the neighborhood from appraiser records or recent public ally published deed conveyances to gain a base knowledge of the value of the property.

5.   Obtain the PLAT MAP showing the specific property dimensions, boundaries and access points.

6.   View the property to confirm the location, status of improvements and any apparent issues that exist.

7.   Calculate the potential additional costs that will be necessary to make the property usable or marketable.

8.   Determine the use that you would make of the property.

9.   Calculate your maximum bid amount including the legal costs, transfer costs and any additional matters that may need to be cleared to gain full use of the property.

A city, county or other public entity may charge amounts that are liened against the property.

Example: Water and sewer services are typically liened against the property rather then the individual ordering and using the services.

At times, these costs may not be abolished as part of the tax sale preparations. In addition to the public records search, you should contact all municipal providers to determine if any outstanding debt still exists that could become your obligation upon the purchase of the property at the tax sale.

DATA GATHERING

PUBLIC RECORDS QUICK LIST

1.   Chain of title to determine all owners of record

2.   All legal action pertaining to all owners of record

3.   Status of mortgages

4.   Status of judgments

5.   Status of all liens that might effect the property

6.   Transfer price of previous sales of the property – shown on deeds of conveyance

PROPERTY ASSESSOR DATA

1.   Assessed Value

2.   Property Address

3.   Legal Description

4.   Current Legal Owner of Record

5. Status of Improvements – to be confirmed by physical inspection

6. Type of Improvements

7. Site Zoning Classification

8. Plat Map

9. Previous Assessment Appraisal Data

PLAT MAP QUICK LIST

1. Property Dimensions

2. Property Shape

3. Access

4. Easements

5. Neighboring Property Information

COMPARABLE SALES DATA AND MLS SYSTEM

1. Sales data indicating the pricing of similar property sold or listed for sale

2. Listing term indicating the time on the market for similar property in the neighborhood

TAX LIEN AND TAX DEED SALES

PROPERTY DATA FORM

Property Address: _____

Map Number: _____   Tax Identification Number: _____

Assessed Value: _____   Zoning: _____

Legal Description

```



```

Site Drawing / Dimensions

```




```

Improvements: _____
_____
_____

Photograph 1	Photograph 2

Figure 12:1 – Sample Property Data Form – Page 1

Current Owner: _____

Current Co-Owner: _____

Lis Pendens Index	Date	Amounts	Status

Mortgage	Date	Amounts	Status

Judgments / Liens	Date	Amounts	Status

Previous Sales/Comparables	Date	Amounts	Notes

Figure 12:2 – Sample Property Data Form – Page 2

UPCOMING SALE DATA COLLECTION – TAX ASSESSOR

COUNTY: _____ TELEPHONE NUMBER: _____

When is the next scheduled tax sale auction?		
How many sales do you offer per year?		
What are the dates of the sales?		
What types of sales are they?		
Where may I obtain a list of the property to be sold?		
What are the registration pre-requites?		
What types of payment do you accept?		
What is the bidding process for the sale?		
May I bid by proxy?	Yes	No
What is the method for bidding by proxy?	Sealed	Phone/Internet
Do you have a web site that contains the list?	Yes	No
Address		
Do you have a web site that enables a preliminary records search?	Yes	No
Web Address		
What happens to liens/deeds that are not sold at the sale?		
Can unsold liens/deeds be purchased from the county after the sale?	Yes	No
What is the process for counter purchases of unsold liens/deeds/		
Are there liens/deeds available over the counter now?	Yes	No
How do I obtain a list of available liens/deeds for over the counter purchase?		
Is there a post-sale redemption period?	Yes	No
How long is the post sale redemption?		
Will I incur additional costs beyond the bid amount when I win a property?	Yes	No
What are these costs?		

Figure 12:3 – Sample Sale Data Form

CHAPTER

13

Planning Your Strategy

*Most of us realize that passive income and the return
generated through the careful investment of our money is
imperative to our future. As more Americans become
concerned with gaining the resources we will need during
our retirement, we have begun looking for a solid, safe
investment opportunity. Tax Deed and Lien Investments
offer such a secure investment arena to an investor willing
to put forth the effort to plan their strategy with care.*

*Real Estate Tax Deeds and Liens offer the ability to create
a real estate empire through the investment of pennies on
the dollar.*

Before beginning the planning of your investment strategy, you should consider the two
types of income you will generate during your life.

The first is **active income**.

* Active income is the income generated by your effort and requiring your actual presence.

- Essentially, to earn this type of income through you exchange work hours for a paycheck.

- This active income is typically sufficient to fund our daily lives.

  Active income pays our bills and sometimes provides for the pleasures we desire in our daily lives.

- This type of income is rarely sufficient to build long-term wealth and security.

- This type of income is typically received on a regulated basis and spent just as quickly.

Recent studies indicate that you should have approximately 5 years worth of base living expenses saved toward retirement by the age of 35.

These same studies show that a goal of $350,000 - $500,000 in liquid assets is a reasonable expectation by the age of 55.

It appears difficult, based upon the average income of $35,600 - $42,500 per year, to generate not only enough income to live today, but to retire comfortably and attain all of our additional dreams and desires in the meantime.

When you plan to use active income to reach all of your goals, you must review your work hour availability against your potential income per hour. It will take many hours of additional effort to earn enough active income to attain the three goals of every worker.

1. Substantiate today's lifestyle   -   pay the bills

2. Reach our dreams   -   afford the extra luxuries in life

3. Enjoy the golden years   -   earn enough income during our active working years to support ourselves in our retirement years

Oftentimes, the active income you can earn through the exchange of your work hours is enough to fulfill one or two of the common goals of every worker but not enough to achieve all three. This need for additional income brings us to the second type of income you must understand and should begin generating in order to reach your goals today and create a stable, secure future for yourself and your family.

This income is known as **passive income**.

- Income earned from investments fall under the category of passive income.

- This income earned through investments does not require your physical presence for its creation.

  When dealing with passive income, your hourly work effort is not being offset by a paycheck.

- To generate passive income, you must strategically invest your current capital in a manner designed to provide a monetary return on that income.

- This type of income will allow you to build wealth and stability.

- This type of income is not contingent upon your employment position, your educational background, the hours in a workweek or the salary your employer is willing to pay for your services.

- The best method of generating passive income is to create a broad portfolio that includes a variety of income streams or types of investments.

- These income streams should be form sources that encompass a variety of risk levels and return percentages.

  This method of investment in passive income is known as diversification.

This course is designed to teach you about one method you should carefully consider in your attempts to diversify your investments to reach your goals through passive income returns. This is the tax lien and tax deed investment.

Tax Lien or Deed Investments

Tax lien certificates and tax deed investments are readily available around the country. The process of selling these certificates and deeds has been in place for generations and the processes continue because they provide each individual involved with the ability to fulfill their needs.

- The taxing authority gains the funds they need to procure the services they promise to provide to their community.

- The investor gains the returns they desire to assist in building the stable future they are striving to attain.

The returns generated through tax certificate investments are fixed by statute. This will result in a stability of the return premium regardless of economic conditions, stock market stability, bank rate returns, and any other factor that affects traditional investment opportunity.

Everyone knows that real estate is an investment that generates a return.

- The quantity of real estate available is finite and therefore the value of real estate continues to increase.

- Real estate values might increase slowly or increase by dramatic amounts but it is assured that real estate values will continue to rise.

Investing in tax deeds is an excellent method of generating passive income. The longer you retain your ownership of the investment property, the more valuable your investment will become and thus the higher the return you can expect of your capital investment.

Before you attend your first sale, it is important that you chart your investment strategy.

To create a personalized investment strategy you must first evaluate your position and then determine your goals.

1. Investment dollars available today

2. Investment goals and needs

3. Term available to reach the investment return necessary to attain the goals

4. Personal investment-risk level assessment

5. Investment possibilities that meet all of your criteria

Example:	Investment dollars available	$3,000
	Investment goals	Long-term return to meet your financial needs during retirement
	Term available to reach goals	15-20 years
	Risk level assessment	Low because every dollar invested must provide a return to meet your long-term goals
	Investment possibility	This type of investment criteria lends itself to the investment in a high-yield tax certificate purchase.

The initial investment capital required for the purchase of a tax certificate is often very low allowing you to generate a decent return well in excess of most market offerings on your smaller initial capital.

The higher yield investments might not provide a full return on your dollars until the redemption period expires fitting with the long-term goals listed in the example.

The return you can expect will be the dollars you invested plus the interest and penalty promised or the deed to an actual piece of real estate worth 10's or even 100's of times the amount of your initial investment.

This provides you with a low risk and higher yield investment return.

When considering this type of investment you will also need to consider the longevity of the goals that you have planned to achieve. If you were to invest in a higher-yield tax certificate, you might plan your long-term strategy in the following manner.

Initial Investment Capital	$3,000
Yield Return	x 25%
	$ 750
Yield Term	1 year

The breakdown indicates that in one year you will earn a return of $750.00 on your $3,000 investment.

- If the lien certificate is not redeemed during the redemption period, you may receive the actual deed to the property.

- If the lien certificate is redeemed during the redemption period, you will gain back all of your initial investment dollars plus the interest that has accumulated on the certificate.

Given your goal term of 15-20 years toward retirement, let us continue the breakdown to determine how well the initial $3,000 in investment capital meets your goals.

Year 1 Investment Capital $ 3,000.00   Return 25%   = $ 750.00

Year 2 Investment Capital $ 3,750.00   Return 25%   = $ 937.50

Year 3 Investment Capital $ 4,687.50   Return 25%   = $ 1,171.88

Year 4 Investment Capital $ 5,859.38   Return 25%   = $ 1,464.85

Year 5 Investment Capital $ 7,324.23   Return 25%   = $ 1,831.06

Year 6 Investment Capital $ 9,155.21   Return 25%   = $ 2,288.82

Year 7 Investment Capital $11,544.03   Return 25%   = $ 2,886.01

Year 8 Investment Capital $14,430.04   Return 25%   = $ 3,607.51

Year 9 Investment Capital $18,037.55   Return 25%   = $ 4,509.39

Year 10 Investment Capital $22,546.94   Return 25%   = $ 5,636.74

Year 11 Investment Capital $28,183.68   Return 25%   = $ 7,045.92

Year 12 Investment Capital $35,229.60   Return 25%   = $ 8,807.40

Year 13 Investment Capital $44,037.00   Return 25%   = $11,009.25

Year 14 Investment Capital $55,046.25   Return 25%   = $13,761.56

Year 15 Investment Capital $68,807.81   Return 25%   = $17,201.95

If you decided to halt the investment planning of expected returns through tax lien certificates at the 15 year mark, you could expect that your initial capital investment of $3,000, consistently capitalized and returned to the investment pool, would bring you a final figure of $86,009.76.

This return on the original investment of $3,000 is unheard of within most investment opportunity. To achieve these results you would simply maintain a consistent level of investment in tax lien certificates with a 1-year redemption and a fixed return of 25%.

Once you have created your return breakdown as described above, you would then determine how this final return at year 15 meets your overall goals. These overall goals will be different for each individual. It is important to make your goals customized to your situation. Many financial analysts are making broad range predictions of financial needs at retirement but only you can determine exactly what level you must reach to retire with comfort and security.

- If your liquid asset goal at year 15 was $75,000 then this investment strategy not only meets, but also surpasses your goals.

- If you investment goal for year 20 is actually to have $300,000 in liquid assets from this particular investment stream, you will see that the capital investment of $3,000 does not meet these needs over the 15 year strategy term.

To meet the needs you must increase your initial investment by $10,500 or determine what other options might be combined with the tax sale- investment strategy that will enable you to reach your goals.

Example: Another example might be if you desire an immediate return of a large amount of capital in exchange for a relatively small investment amount.

This return might provide you with the capital you need to invest higher initial funds in future sales. This higher investment plan would make your ultimate long-term strategy easier to reach.

In other words, if you take the same $3,000 investment capital described above, invest in a tax deed property worth $30,000 you might make an immediate return at the sale of the property of $27,000.

The initial $3,000 of personal capital could be returned to your original account or paid back to the funding source.

The profit of $27,000 could be invested allowing you to gain a return using passively earned income rather than risk your own actively earned income.

SAMPLE AFTER RETURN OF INITIAL INVESTMENT CAPITAL

Year 1 Investment Capital	$ 27,000.00	x Return 25%	=	$ 6750.00
Year 2 Investment Capita	1 $ 33,750.00	x Return 25%	=	$ 8437.50
Year 3 Investment Capital	$ 42,187.50	x Return 25%	=	$ 10,546.88
Year 4 Investment Capital	$ 52,734.38	x Return 25%	=	$ 13,183.60
Year 5 Investment Capital	$ 65,917.98	x Return 25%	=	$ 16,479.50
Year 6 Investment Capital	$ 82,387.48	x Return 25%	=	$ 20,599.37
Year 7 Investment Capital	$102,986.85	x Return 25%	=	$ 25,746.71
Year 8 Investment Capital	$128,733.56	x Return 25%	=	$ 32,183.39
Year 9 Investment Capital	$160,916.95	x Return 25%	=	$ 40,229.24
Year 10 Investment Capital	$201,146.18	x Return 25%	=	$ 50,286.55

Year 11 Investment Capital	$251,432.72	x Return 25%	=	$ 62,858.18
Year 12 Investment Capital	$314,290.90	x Return 25%	=	$ 78,572.73
Year 13 Investment Capital	$392,863.63	x Return 25%	=	$ 98,215.91
Year 14 Investment Capital	$491,079.54	x Return 25%	=	$122,769.88
Year 15 Investment Capital	$613,849.42	x Return 25%	=	$153,462.35

The calculations above show the return you could achieve if you invested $3,000 into a tax deed that yielded a profit of $27,000. The initial investment would then be returned to the funding source and all profit would be reinvested in a 1-year redemption, 25% tax lien certificate each year over a 15-year strategy period. The final total from the investment would equal $767,311.77 at year 15..

You should carefully consider your goals, fund availability, and level of acceptable risk before entering the tax sale arena. Both deed and certificate sales present an incredible opportunity for the well-informed investor. By completing your investment strategy before attending the sale, you will promote a more secure and satisfying investment result.

Now that you have defined your needs from the investments you plan to make, it is time to choose a sale to attend.

The first step in choosing a sale is to determine the rate of return you require.

- If you attend a deed sale then the rate of return you can expect from your investment will be calculated using the fair market value from recent home sales in the area of the investment property you plan to purchase. Many States now have the MLS system that will show you the listing prices for homes in your area using a simple search method. If you do not have an online MLS database, a local Real Estate Agent will be able to provide you with a printout listing that provide comparison homes for your review.

- If you attend a certificate sale, the rate of return will depend on the State and County of the sale you attend. The rate of return is set by area and you can obtain a general idea of the expected rate by reviewing the State guide contained in the next chapter. Before attending the sale, you should contact the County Tax Assessment office to confirm that the rate has not been changed since the creation of the quick chart included in this program.

In addition to the rate promised by the taxing authority, you must consider the probability that you will receive the payment from the owner of record. The economic condition within the County will provide strong indicators as to the likelihood of the owner redeeming the certificate. If you are attending certificate sales, you are typically looking to obtain a cash return not the property deed. As such, you must factor the probability of owner payment into your strategy.

- If you invest in a tax certificate in an area that has a high rate of unemployment and a repressed real estate market, you would be less likely to receive payment from the owner.

- If you invest in a tax certificate in an area that is showing a more stable economy and regular growth, it will be more likely that the owner will redeem his lien certificate.

This qualifying factor should influence your investment location as strongly if not more strongly than the posted rate of return. It will not benefit you to purchase a tax certificate that promises a 50% return on your investment if the economy where the property is located is so repressed that the owner of record is unable to make any payments toward the certificate.

The final consideration that should be factored into your strategy is the type of property you will choose for your investment. We have discussed tax deed and tax lien investments but within these investments are sub-categories that are based on the usage or zoning classification of the property.

The primary zoning classifications include Residential, Commercial, Developable Land, and Agricultural. Each of these classification carries with it different benefits and drawbacks. Some of the perceived benefits or drawbacks will be influenced by your investment strategy. The property location and regional economic conditions will influence other possible benefits or drawbacks.

Residential
Residential property carries with it some of the most obvious benefits and drawbacks. Most of us understand residential real estate better than we do other types of property. The residential real estate investment provides many obvious options following the obtainment of a tax deed.

Uses

- Restore the property to prime condition and list it for immediate resale.

- Restore the property to prime condition and use it to generate rental real estate income.

- Restore the property to prime condition and sell it using a creative finance technique to increase the income potential through interest accumulation while minimizing the costs and time investment that might occur with rental real estate.

- Retain the property for personal use thereby minimizing the costs of your primary living space and allowing you to use the funds that would otherwise go toward a mortgage payment to invest in other, future real estate tax deeds.

Cautions

- It is difficult, without gaining access to the property, to determine the condition of the investment prior to the date of the sale. It is possible that you will acquire a property and discover that the restoration activity you must complete to make it a usable investment costs tens or even thousands of dollars.

- You should always verify the location of the property you are considering. Purchasing a property that is in a poor neighborhood or contains other environmental issues might lower the potential value and possible uses.

- You should always complete a comprehensive investigation into the title of any real estate purchase you plan to make. Residential real estate is the most common type of real estate to carry easements, liens, judgments, and breaks in the chain of title or other matters. If you attend a sale that is considered subject to, you might be required to invest further time and money in clearing these issues before you can gain any return from your new investment.

Commercial

Commercial property can be an incredible opportunity. It is typical that a piece of property zoned for commercial or industrial uses will be far more valuable than a standard residential investment making the potential return probability higher for the investor.

Uses

- Restore the property and offer it for sale within the area.

- Restore or re-construct the property and offer the rental of all or parts of the property to one or more businesses within the area.

- Attempt to transfer the property to the government for use as an industrial or commercial growth program. Many communities suffering from a poor economy are seeking property to offer as part of a development program.

- Hold the property in anticipation of the completion of some future, planned event such as the opening of a new business park or the creation of new roads. These events often cause commercial use property values to increase rapidly. If you are aware of a planned event and are able to hold the property until this event occurs, the potential return could be drastically increased.

Cautions

- The market for commercial or industrial use property is more limited than for residential real estate. This means that the potential pool of buyers is lower and the property might take longer to sell on the general market than other possible investments.

- The economy plays an even larger role in the sale or rent of a commercial use property. You should carefully review the stability of the market and even the neighborhood in which the property is located. A growing or heavily industrialized area will likely bring you a reasonable purchase offer within a fast period. However, if the property is located in an area that is having difficulty maintaining the current businesses then the probability of growth and therefore the quantity of potential buyers for your property will be lower.

- It is important to consider the possible environmental issues that may have developed during prior usage of the commercial or industrial property. Many investors have purchased what they believed was a prime piece of real estate only to discover that tens of thousands of dollars must be invested to make the land environmentally safe for future use. There are grants and other options available from both the government and private foundations for the clean up of environmentally hazardous parcels of land; however, the competition for these funds is often high. The time investment of such a clean-up effort should also be considered.

- The taxes assessed against a commercial or industrial use property are often high compared to a standard residential investment. This is due to the increased value of the property that, at first glance, appears to be a positive feature. However, during the term that you hold ownership of a commercial or industrial property, you will be responsible for the payment of the assessed taxes. If the property requires an extended time investment in order to sell, the eventual return on your investment will be lowered with each day you hold the property.

- The rental of a commercial or industrial use property will often bring a higher monthly income than a standard residential investment; however, there are often additional costs that must be considered. You will probably need to purchase an owner's insurance policy to protect you in the event of an injury or other matter affecting the property. These are often more costly than a residential owner's policy. You might also find it necessary to develop a corporation or other management company to protect your personal assets and minimize the impact that any financial suit against the industry to which you rent might have on your personal financial position. These additional considerations will incur costs and the probable costs must be factored into your investment return plan.

Developable Land

The purchase of raw land that can be developed at some future time is a cost effective, long-term investment that suits many strategies. Land typically carries a lower taxation rate and appreciates over time. In addition, raw land often sells for far less at the tax sale than other pieces of developed property. This lower up-front cost might allow you to purchase more property today and begin building a portfolio of property that will assist you in meeting your long-term investment strategy faster.

Uses

- You might purchase raw land that is within an area that is considered desirable. If this occurs and the area is currently being developed, you could sell the land at a profit immediately.

- The plans for the community in which you are making your investment will play a large role in the use you make of any raw land purchase. If you are aware of a planned expansion, community or new development in a particular area you may want to purchase land that is within or just outside of the area of planned development. The purchase of land just outside the planned expansion provides you with the opportunity to hold the land until the expansion comes to your property and increases the final value.

- If land is within an area that provides water and sewer as well as other utility, you could rent the land to an individual looking to erect a temporary home. This may generate additional costs for you to gain the access to the needed utility but allows you to hold the land parcel for a future increase in value while obtaining a steady income flow immediately.

Cautions

- The zoning of the land investment you make will play a role in the possible uses. Commercial, residential, agricultural and special use land all have different potential and you should carefully consider the eventual market.

- The location and research into the public records of raw land is imperative prior to making such an investment. Easements, lack of right of way, encroachments, and flood hazards are all considerations that you should research before making such an investment. A piece of land that cannot be accessed will typically not be an easy parcel to sell. If an easement is held by another party against the land then it may be difficult to make total use of the land. At times, development might be virtually impossible unless the easement can be removed. If the land is located in a flood plain then development on that parcel might be prohibited by statute. Even if development rights are not inhibited, the flood insurance that most lenders will require any owner who uses that land for an improvement to carry can be costly and will limit the potential buyers you will be able to locate.

These possible uses and cautions are only the most common that you should consider. You will want to research any investment property you consider before risking your money on the transaction. It is important that you review the community, uses, drawbacks, and benefits of every investment you make as if your last dollar hinged on the successful use of that investment. This view will enable you to make the correct decision at every sale and will help to minimize the risks that you may encounter with Tax Deed and Tax Lien investments.

MONEY, MONEY, MONEY

When you are creating your investment plan, sourcing money to invest in the tax sales will be one of the fundamentals that you must consider. There is incredible opportunity and profit potential in tax sale investments, but you must gain access to seed capital to begin to obtain your piece of the profit. If you are an investor who has a ready supply of cash to begin, then future sales, redemptions and rental of the property you purchase should allow you to grow your investment fund rapidly. If you are reading this coursework and do not have seed capital, then tax sale investment might seem like a dream for someday in the future. The good news is that there is money available, you just need to sit down with your finances and locate your source.

If you already own a home, obtaining a line of credit against the equity in the home might be an option for gaining the funds to begin your investment process. A line of credit is a revolving line secured against your property. Because this line is well secured, the interest rate that you will be required to pay will often be lower than that offered through a personal loan or a credit card. The other benefit to a revolving line of credit is that you typically make interest payments only on the amount of money you owe at a given time. If you do not own your own home, you may still obtain a line of credit but an unsecured line will carry a higher interest rate and so the return must surpass the interest that will accrue on the funds you borrow.

Example: Open the line of credit

Line of Credit Available $20,000
Line of Credit Used $ 0
Monthly interest penalty @10% $ 0

Tax sale approaches
Line of Credit Available $20,000
Credit dispersed for tax sale $ 5,500
Monthly interest penalty @10% $ 45.83

Many revolving lines allow for interest only payments. This would mean that you are only required to pay the actual interest on the principal each month.

If you chose that route with the above example, your monthly outgo for the privilege of using the borrowed funds would be $45.83.

Conversely, many revolving lines allow the borrower to pay interest only on the amount of money they owe so if you make a Principal and Interest payment each month, the interest penalty figure will decrease with each payment.

You should use a financial calculator to help you determine the best and most profitable method of borrower and repaying funds from a line of credit such as this compared to your investment strategy. For instance, if you have purchased a tax deed at a free and clear sale, you will be able to make use of the property much more quickly than if, you purchase at an upset sale. This being the case, it may make the most sense to your cash flow to make interest only payments until such time as you either sell or rent the property thus enabling you to use other peoples money to pay off the debt against the property.

If you have purchased a tax lien certificate whose interest penalty is 18%, you might want to consider paying down the line of credit as soon as possible to enable you to gain the highest return on your investment. It is still a good profit to pay 10% to the lender and receive a return of 18% from the delinquent property owner so your investment needs and desires will play a large part in determining what method of repayment will work best for you.

CREDIT CARDS

Credit cards are typically readily available to you for investment purposes. Many provide direct check deposit offerings or cash advance options that will enable you to gain access to the funds available on your account quickly and without a great deal of excess paperwork or time investment. While this can be a benefit when you are starting the investment process, you must factor the higher rates often attached to credit cards and the percentage fee that credit card companies will sometimes charge for the cash advance or use of the checks against your line. It may still be a benefit to use available credit from your credit cards for investment purposes, but you should carefully consider the penalties and interest that will accumulate on the investment funds you are borrowing.

You may be able to play the transfer balance game for a time and access low interest credit but will still incur the transaction penalty, which averages 3% among most cards.

It is important that you have a sound strategy for gaining possession, clear title and use of your investment property before choosing to use funds advanced from your credit card.

Tax lien sales will present an even larger dilemma if you plan to gain your investment capital from a credit card. The interest rate you obtain on the certificate lien must be enough to offset any interest charges that will accumulate on the credit card advance PLUS any transaction fees that you may incur to gain access to the cash of the credit line or to transfer balances in the pursuit of primer or starter rate offers.

LIQUIDATE CURRENT ASSETS

If you are currently in the real estate market, you may have other investments available that you could refinance, sell or lease option. This would gain a lump sum of cash that you will be able to invest in tax sales. You should review your portfolio to determine which property might be ripe for a refinance or is lower producing and might be an excellent liquidation option.

SEEK BUSINESS FUNDING

Another option that might be available to you is to obtain funding from an SBA lender in your area. Entering the tax sale arena is, in essence, a business opportunity. If you are able to convert your general strategy into an exceptional business plan that shows how you will use the funds lent through an SBA loan, they might be able to provide you with ready cash to invest in a tax deed plus funding for the required restoration work to any property that you purchase. It is vital that you learn the fundamentals of business plan generation before you approach a lender with a request to borrow in this manner. If you have a local SCORE chapter in your area, you might want to consider beginning the process of creating your business plan there. SCORE is a group of retired business people from a specific area who donate their time and knowledge base to assist other small businesses in gaining a foothold in their area.

CREATE A PARTNERSHIP

At times, you may be able to locate a partner to assist you with the tax sale process. You are completing this course and have gained knowledge of the steps, best practices and methodology behind tax sale investment. This knowledge is what you can bring to the partnership. If you can locate a contractor, family or friend, businessperson or venture capitalist who is excited by the potential in tax sale investments but lacking in the knowledge that you have gained, you might be able to work a partnership where you supply the legwork and brainpower and they supply the funds!

These are the most common methods that we have assisted investors in employing to gain access to funds. Your situation, investment goals and strategy will dictate the best method of gaining seed capital for your new venture. If you have a retirement fund, exceptional credit history, high unused line on your credit card, equity in your home or other real estate your choices will be different from the next individual.

CHAPTER 14

Sale Process

*Congratulations! You have reached the chapter that
marks your obtainment of the knowledge and skills that
you need to reach for your dreams and conquer wealth
through successful tax sale investment. You are now ready
to enter the sale of your choice, make competent
investment decisions and purchase the deed or lien that
will assist you in reaching your investment goals and
achieving your dreams. Upon completion of this chapter,
choose your sale venue, research the potential investments,
attend the sale and win!*

On the day of the sale, you will enter the location dictated by the list that you have been using to screen investments, research potential pitfalls and plan your investment strategy.

Each sale will have bidding pre-requisites that you must meet and the actual form of the sale may vary. Some sales will require attendance by any individual who is planning to bid while others enable bidders to bid by proxy. Bidding will also vary by the type of sale that you attend. It is important that you plan to attend a sample sale prior to attending for buying a tax lien or tax deed. This sample sale will enable you to finalize your education and prepare for your first purchase. At the sample sale, you should determine the methodology and requirements set by statute and will want to observe the other bidders. Observing the actions and interests of the bidders who attend the sale you will use to reach your goals will enable you to determine the popularity of the sale you have chosen as the venue for starting your investment career. You will also be able to make base assessments pertaining to the investment strategy, bid limitations of each regular attendee, and generate a strategy based upon the common bid actions of those attending the sale.

- Upon entry into the sale location, you will be asked to complete a series of sale registration forms and pre-requisites.

  These forms provide the information the Tax Claim Office will use in the creation of your tax deed or certificate.

  Common pre-requisites are the certificate of your true name and address as well as the completion of a statement indicating you are not past-due in any tax billing.

- Once you have completed and remitted the applicable registration forms, you will receive a bidding number that will enable you to bid on the property offered during the sale.

- You will be required to certify that you meet certain requirements set for bidders at that sale. These will vary by Jurisdiction but should include some of the following criteria.

  > A bidder must be lawfully allowed and competent to conduct real estate transactions.

  > No individual may bid if he or she is in arrears on any monies owed to the Tax Assessment Bureau, Municipality or other authority.

- You must provide valid identification showing that you are the person you claim to be.

- You will sign a notice indicating that you accept the terms and conditions of the sale.

- The final list of property available to be purchased and a notice of the sale instructions and limitations will be provided to you.

  All bidders must review this notice and remit a statement showing that they fully understand the limitations expressed by the Tax Claim Bureau as to the sale, the liability of the Tax Claim Bureau and the condition of the property or title to the property.

- The day of the sale, you should also receive a notice of TERMS AND CONDITIONS for the sale that illustrate all conditions of the sale and provide you with additional information regarding the sale and the interest being sold.

  An example of a TERMS AND CONDITIONS disclosure you might encounter included on the following page.

TERMS AND CONDITIONS

The following conditions shall govern the sale of properties by the Tax Claim Bureau for delinquent taxes scheduled for <u>DATE</u> or to such other dates to which the sale may be adjourned or continued.

1. All properties are sold under and by virtue of Section _____ as amended of the Act of _____ known as the real estate tax sale law.

2. The Tax Claim Bureau will sell the property as described on the dockets of record and make not representation or warranty as to the description nor will it make any survey on a property sold. There are no warranties on the marketability of the title acquired.

3. The Tax Claim Bureau will sell (subject to/not subject to) existing tenancies and record liens.

   This disclosure notice will vary depending on the type of sale you are attending. A judicial sale is typically conducted as a free and clear sale and is not subject to other discovered liens. An upset sale is typically a sale for only the taxable interest in the property and may be conducted subject to other liens as exist in record.

4. The purchaser shall pay by either cash or certified check. No property scheduled for sale will be knocked down unless the bid is equal to or more than the minimum upset price of the property to be sold. In the event of a dispute by the bidders or failure to pay by the winning bidder the purchase price and deed costs as well as the recording fee and realty transfer tax immediately after the sale, the property will be put up for resale. This will be done, if necessary, later in the Tax Claim Office.

5. All properties sold are under and subject to entry fees as fixed by the Recorder of Deeds and Prothonotory. The purchaser must pay these immediately after the purchase price is paid. In addition to the purchase price, the purchaser must pay the following: Recording fee $0.00 and Transfer tax of 0%. The 0% transfer tax is 0% of the assessed valuation of the property as adjusted by the common factor ratio. The purchase price along with a $0.00 deed cost s well as the recording fees are payable at: _____.

Figure 14:1 – Sample Sale Terms and Conditions Disclosures – Page 1

6. All sales are subject to confirmation by the Court of Common Pleas of the County and will be submitted to the court no later than sixty days after the date of the sale.

7. The Tax Claim Bureau will issue a deed/certificate as applicable to the purchaser upon confirmation by the court. The deed will not contain any warranty, either general or special. The Tax Claim Bureau will record the deed. Approximately four months from the date of the sale is needed before the original deed will be returned to the purchaser following its recordation.

8. The purchaser of any property at the upset sale will be responsible for the next year real estate taxes. In the event the purchaser does not receive a tax statement, they should contact the tax collector in that district to insure payment of taxes during the interim period in which the record changes in ownership is taking place.

PLEASE NOTE: No owner of record can bid on his or her own property.

BUYERS BEWARE: The tax claim bureau is selling the property without any guarantee or warranty whatever, either as to structures or lack of structures upon the land, liens, title or any other matter or thing whatever.

PLEASE NOTE: Any party submitting the final bid who refuses or neglects to pay the bid amount will be held liable for payment of the entire amount plus the associated costs.

The sale will commence at the pre-determined time regardless of the presence and registration completion of all bidders. You should ensure you arrive at the sale before the opening time as posted in the list notices and published in the newspaper. This ensures you will have adequate time to complete the registration process and obtain a bidder number before the opening of the bidding on the property.

Figure 14:2 – Sample Sale Terms and Conditions Disclosures – Page 2

Tax sales are held in the auction style format. This means the auctioneer designated to lead the auction will open the bidding at a certain amount. The methodology of bidding activity will depend on the type of sale that you attend.

- Some bidding starts at the amount equal to the upset costs of the past due taxes plus penalties, interest and any other assessments required for the purchase of the property deed or certificate.

- Some sales follow an assessed value bidding method where additional value amounts will be incorporated into the opening bid amount.

- Some sales will follow the reverse bidding methodology where the maximum acceptable amount is the starting bid and all bidders will bid down until only one winning bidder remains.

The methodology commonly followed at the sales will depend on the type of sale you attend as well as the regional variations written into the statute of the applicable sale. You should review the method that will be employed at the sale you plan to attend so that the format is familiar to you when you begin the actual bidding process.

- **Traditional Auction Style**

  All bids start at the base price set by the taxing authority

  Bidding progresses following traditional auction style format

  All interested bidders raise the bid in increments until only one-bidder remains

  The highest bidder wins the tax deed

- **Traditional Premium Bidding**

  All bids start at the maximum certificate interest rate as set by statute

  Premium starts at 0%

  The highest premium bid wins the tax certificate

- **Circle Bidding**

  All interested investors sit in a circle

  The tax collector proceeds around the circle offering the property according to the list form to the next bidder in the circle

  The bidder accepts the property or passes it to the next investor in line

  If no bidders accept the property, the tax collector moves onto the next property on the list

If a bidder accepts the property, the next property on the list is offered to the next investor in line

The offering process continues in a circular form until all of the property being offered at the sale has been offered to the investors

This process is not used as frequently and must be agreed upon by all investors attending the sale prior to the commencement of bidding

- **Sealed Bid Process**

    All interested investors complete the registration process in advance of the sale

    The investor determines the pre-set bid amount they are willing to pay for each property

    The investor sends the bids to the Tax Collector in a sealed envelope

    The Tax Collector opens all of the remitted bids at the pre-set date and time

    The highest bidder wins the bid

Regardless of the formatting of the bidding process, the interested bidders will signal their desire to bid on the property by either raising their bid card or paddle or calling out the next bid they are willing to place.

Bidding will continue in this manner until one individual's bid is not raised by another bidder at the auction. The final bidder will be the winner, however some sales will take note of the secondary bidder. In the event the winning bidder fails to finalize the transaction, the secondary bidder may be offered the property.

Certain states have a proxy bidding system in place that allows for bidding by individuals not physically present at the auction. Proxy bidding may be accomplished using various methods and the allowable bidding methods will be set by statute.

- A proxy bidder may document a preset maximum bid on a particular parcel or property in writing and provide this to the authorized auction representative before the beginning of the sale. This is typically called a sealed bid.

- A proxy bidder may maintain a live telephone bid option with an authorized representative of the proceedings. In this method, the bidder is pre-registered and offers bids by telephone via the proxy during the actual bidding at the sale.

Some States now offer direct Internet bidding during the open auction proceedings. This process works in a manner similar to that of the telephone bid proxy except it is conducted via live Internet link with the authorized proxy.

Upon the acceptance by the authorized auctioneer of the highest and final bid on a parcel or property, a representative authorized by the court records the bidding number and final bid amount for each sold parcel. This person is typically a Recorder but may be any individual authorized to perform this function. The lists generated by this individual will be used to finalize payments, generate sale receipts and eventually, to finalize the certificate or deed to the property that has been purchased.

If a property is not sold at the designated auction, the Tax Claim Bureau has a variety of options available with regard to the unsold listings. The use of these options may present an additional investment opportunity for you.

- The Tax Claim Bureau may continue the auction to another date and time to provide an additional opportunity for bidders to purchase the unsold parcels or certificates.

- The Tax Claim Bureau may choose to continue the lien against the property, adding additional assessments, penalties and interest and attempt to sell the property at the next scheduled tax sale proceeding.

- The Tax Claim Bureau may provide the property owner or other interested party with another period of redemption during which they may redeem their title. They will accomplish the redemption by paying all funds as deemed due and payable by the Taxing Authority and as set forth by Statute and Jurisdictional regulations.

At the end of the sale, successful bidders will proceed to the location set for payments of the winning bids and other costs associated with the transfer of the tax interest in the property sold. The payment location will vary by region but it is often conducted in the Tax Assessment Offices of the County Courthouse.

- Most sales require payment be made by either cash or certified check.

- The successful bidder is expected to make payment on their bid and other required costs immediately following the sale.

Upon finalizing the payment promised and receiving your tax receipt or lien certificate, you will have successfully completed the purchase portion of the tax sale process.

Following the sale there will be specific actions a successful bidder may take. These actions will vary depending on the type of sale, the term of confirmation by the courts required after the sale and the status of the high bidder as either a deed holder or tax certificate holder.

When the sale is over and you have successfully invested in a piece of tax real estate, and have obtained the deed or a lien certificate there are still processes you must follow. These processes will lead to a return on your investment.

We have reviewed three basic methods of investment.

- The free and clear tax deed

- The lienable tax deed

- The tax lien certificate

Each of these three methods of investment requires different actions on your part to assist you in realizing your return.

FREE AND CLEAR/JUDICIAL TAX DEED SALE

We illustrated earlier that the free and clear title of the judicial sale is sometimes a misnomer. The Terms and Conditions example illustrated this point further by detailing the exceptions and specific instructions applicable to the sales.

The taxing authorities do not warrant that the title is free and clear, they simply state that the title has been cleared to the best of their ability. What this means to you is that there is a high probability that the title is free of lien defects but there is no warranty that this is so.

- You should always perform your due diligence to confirm the activity of the taxing authority.

Following a successful bid at the free and clear sale, the transfer of the deed will need to be confirmed by the court and recorded within the public records.

The taxing authority allows themselves a certain period to accomplish these tasks and the waiting period will be defined in the procedure materials governing that particular tax sale. These procedures will usually be provided to each bidder either before or at the sale.

Following the waiting period of between 10 and 180 days, the deed is recorded in your name, copied, and filed in the applicable record book and the original deed is returned to you.

- You are now the owner of record on that parcel or property.

- You are responsible for any taxes or other costs assessed against the property from the day of the sale forward and should ensure you receive the applicable billings as expected.

  If you do not receive future tax bills, assessments or other billings that you believe will be placed against the property, you should contact the billing authority and update the owner of record information to ensure you do not the become a defaulted owner at the next sale.

- You are now the owner of record and have all of the rights to the title and property that were granted to the previous owner.

- You are also subject to any tenancies, agreements, contracts, easements or other encumbrances not removed or abolished by the taxing authorities.

  The defaulted owner, if still occupying the property, will then occupy it in a tenancy or leasehold manner. You will need to go through the appropriate eviction procedure for your jurisdiction to obtain physical possession of your new property.

- Once the property is free of illegal occupants, it is yours to do with, as you desire. Just as in any real estate transfer, you will take possession of the property. You will then perform any upgrades, renovations, or repairs to the property that you see fit.

  - You have the ability to move into the property.

  - You may rent the property subject to the applicable rental regulations.

  - You may offer the property for sale in the real estate market and obtain retail value cash out for your investment.

  - You can even finance the property using creative finance methods, selling it to an individual or entity to receive the down payment, monthly principal and interest payments.

The options now available to you are the same as those provided to any other owner of real estate in your region.

SUBJECT TO UPSET SALE

An upset sale is a tax sale where the property is being sold subject to all existing liens, encumbrance, tenancies, and other defects of title.

You are acquiring the level of ownership interest held by the defaulted owner and nothing more. In this type of sale, the taxing authority does not attempt to research the title to the property or to remove or abolish any defect.

It is your responsibility, as the investor, to determine the exact condition of the title and what, if any, additional liabilities might be held against the property.

There may be no liens, encumbrances or other defects in the title. Multiple matters might exist that will affect your property ownership.

This is where the due diligence performed by the investor plays a key role.

- If you have preformed or caused to have performed a comprehensive search into the public records system, inspected the property for access, interest and occupancy as well as researched the other items shown in this course you will be aware of existing blemishes against the property.

At times, you may acquire the property free of any defect.

- If the property is free of any liens, encumbrances or other blemishes to the title, you are actually obtaining a deed similar to that of the free and clear deed.

The difference between this type of sale and the free and clear sale is that in this type of sale is that the taxing authorities have not attempted to determine this issue for you, the investor.

If you have acquired a deed to a property that is free and clear of any liens, you are still responsible for any easements, tenancies and other matters that may exist. You must ensure you comply with statute concerning these issues. Providing you have complied with all pre-existing conditions in the title or performed the applicable court action to remove these conditions you may take possession of the property.

Upon taking possession of the property the land and improvements to the land are yours to keep, transfer, rent, or other activities just as with a conventionally transferred piece of real estate.

A second scenario for the Subject To sale is that there do exist, in record, additional liens or judgments against the property for which you have taken the tax deed.

If additional defects exist, you have one of two choices available.

- You may institute a foreclosure proceeding and require the property be sold at public sale to regain your investment and return.

It is important to remember when instituting a foreclosure sale that the tax liens always take priority over any other type of lien against the property. This is true regardless of the order of time.

What this means is that you, as the holder of the tax lien deed, will be paid first out of funds received at the foreclosure proceeding. Any other lien holder will be paid out of the remaining proceeds. If another lien holder instigates a foreclosure proceeding before you, the tax-lien deed holder, you will still have the opportunity to be paid.

It is important to determine any proceedings filed against the property or property owner to ensure you have the opportunity to inform all parties of your ownership interest in the property and subsequently obtain payment for your ownership interest.

- In some cases the liens, judgments or other assessments against the property may be relatively small in comparison with the overall value of the property. In these circumstances, you may institute a foreclosure to obtain your cash return and generate sale income from the property to pay these liens, judgments or other matters or you may choose to handle these costs yourself.

If the liens, judgments and other defects against the title are relatively small, you have the opportunity, as the tax deed owner, to pay these costs, as the previous owner would have in the general market transfer of the property.

Once these costs are paid and other defects of title are cleared you are will be the only owner of record to that particular property. As the only owner of record you are then able to keep, sell or otherwise dispose of make use of the property just as any owner of real estate is able.

➤ You can sell the property to make a cash return.

➤ You may choose to occupy the property as your primary residence.

➤ You may choose to use the property as a residential or commercial rental property in compliance with statute and jurisdictional regulations.

➤ You can even sell the property using creative finance techniques to increase the return you obtain from your investment.

Tax Deed Post Sale Processes

- After you have purchased a tax deed at auction, you must wait for the stipulated redemption period of the jurisdiction in which you have chosen to bid.

This redemption period could range from 0 to 3 years depending on your area and you will want to verify any redemption terms prior to placing a bid at the auction.

During the redemption period, the delinquent taxpayer is actually still the owner of the property and your interest is considered a lien on the property.

You will still receive interest or penalty income on your investment but the owner has the right to redeem the property through payment of all obligations to you, the holder of the tax deed certificate.

- If no redemption period exists, you may immediately begin to implement your plans for the property based upon your investment strategy.

- It is important to remember that you must still have a quiet title suit completed on the property.

A quiet title suit is a legal process that notifies the public of the transfer of the property and gives any interested parties who believe they still hold a lien or other matter against the title the opportunity to come forth and present their case.

If you have completed all of the research recommended in the previous chapters, this suit should hold no surprises for you.

To complete a quiet title suit, you should contact a real estate attorney, Title Company or other trustworthy individual who specializes in handling this type of matter.

You can complete the process on your own behalf, but many investors find that the first few attempts are better handled by an outside party.

Once you have completed the process a few times under the guidance of an attorney, you might feel confident enough confidence to complete the process yourself.

- Another option to the full quiet title suit is to contact any individual who has an interest in the property as shown during your research within the public records. You may attempt to obtain a quitclaim deed from each individual named.

A quitclaim deed simply relinquishes any rights the individual might have had in the property.

The quitclaim deed does not state that they hold any specific interest; it simply assists in clearing any ambiguity pertaining to the title and possible interests held.

If the title search showed minimal interests, this might be a more cost effective and speedy method of clearing the title to the property and is one that you should consider.

- Before taking either step, you should consult with a competent real estate attorney to determine what method you should employ to protect your rights in your new property.

  Upon retention by you, the attorney will start a lawsuit to Quiet Title. During this process, the attorney will order a list of individuals who should be served notice of this suit from a Title Company. Notice will be given to anyone who had or had an interest in the property.

  Each of these individuals will be served. The method of service required will vary by jurisdiction and could be personal service, service by certified mail or service by publication in public newspaper.

  Any individual served during this process will have a stipulated time to present their response to the notices.

  ➢ In many cases, the notices will go unanswered and any interest these individuals may have brought forth will be considered defaulted.

    This is the most common response to the notices of this type.

  ➢ If someone answers the notice, a hearing will be set.

    The objections to the suit that this person has will be heard and judged in the court.

    If the individual has a valid right to the property, you must either make a deal to abolish this right or work with the individual to share interest in the property. More often, the individual will be judged to have no interests and the judge will hand down a decision in your favor thereby abolishing any future claims that might be brought by the objecting individuals.

- If a tax deed was purchased at a judicial sale, the foreclosure process completed by the courts will typically remove most items that might have existed against the title.

- If the deed was purchased at an upset sale, your research should show most items that might arise during the quiet title suit.

- The most common result of a quiet title notification is that any individuals served during the process will make no objections. Often, the rights they may have held have been abolished during the process and thus they have no case to bring forth to the judge. When everyone notified during the suit defaults, or fails to bring forth an issue, the attorney will file for a final judgment that declares that the title is quieted.

- Upon receipt of the final judgment, you should begin to implement your strategy for making use of the property. You can rehab the property, rent it, list it for sale or even move into the property and make it your personal residence. The choices are virtually endless and upon completion of a quiet title suit, you own the property free of all liens and encumbrances!

TAX LIEN CERTIFICATE SALE

Following a successful bid at a tax lien sale, you will receive a certificate showing your investment interest in the property. In most states, the assessor's office will record your personal information and interest in the property within the court records to ensure your investment is redeemed should the owner or other interested party redeem the tax certificate or if a sale or other transfer of the property is attempted.

In this type of system, the assessor or tax claims bureau will collect any money paid against the certificate on your behalf.

- The owner or other interested party goes to the applicable office, makes payment, and receives a receipt or a redemption certificate.

- The applicable office then locates the record regarding the investor who holds the certificate and sends you notice of payment.

- If the owner or other interested party has redeemed the entire certificate, you will need to return your lien certificate to the assessor or treasurer offices applicable in your state.

- Upon receipt of the certificate the treasurer, assessor or tax claims authority removes your lien against the property and forwards the applicable payment to you.

- In some cases, the owner or other interested party will only pay a portion of the monies owed. In this situation, the procedures are designated by statute.

  ➢ Some authorities will hold the money in an escrow until the full payment is obtained.

  ➢ Other jurisdictions will issue propionate redemption. In this type of scenario, the redemption certificate you hold must be modified to reflect the decrease in monies owed.

- You will provide the certificate to the proper offices; they will modify the certificate to reflect the new balance. You will receive the funds paid toward the certificate by the owner or other interested party.

- In some cases, neither the owner of record nor other interested party will redeem the lien certificate you hold. In these cases, once the redemption period set by jurisdictional statute expires you have the opportunity to obtain the deed to the actual parcel or property.

- The requirements for converting the tax lien certificate to a tax deed vary by state and by specific jurisdiction.

- In many states there are two, fixed redemption periods.

    When the first redemption period expires, you are able to instigate a foreclosure proceeding to obtain the return of your investment dollars and any interest earned on the investment.

    At the foreclosure proceeding, tax liens will typically take priority over any other lien held against the property. This increases the likelihood of obtaining a return on your investment.

    Some investors choose not to begin foreclosure proceedings at the first redemption period. These investors are typically hoping to gain the cash return on their investment.

    If the certificate holder does not instigate foreclosure proceedings, the taxing authority typically sets a second redemption period that allows the owner additional time to pay the debt to you before losing all interest in their property.

- Once the second redemption period has expired, most states allow the investor to petition the court to convert the tax lien certificate into a tax deed.

    This process would then provide you with full ownership rights to the property subject to existing liens, encumbrances and other title blemishes.

- You can then take possession of the property according to the regulations in your jurisdiction.

    Live in it.

    Sell it on the general market.

    Rent it.

    Even sell the property using creative technique.

CAUTIONS

When holding a tax lien certificate there is another possibility, of which you will need to be aware. We advised you to research the chain of title to any potential investment regardless of the type of investment or interest you will obtain.

If you hold the tax lien certificate against a property that has other liens that are in default the other parties with an interest in the property may institute a foreclosure or judgment sale against the property. They are requesting the sale in an attempt to collect the money they are owed and that is secured against the property.

The fact that another party is implementing a foreclosure proceeding does not negate your interest in the property and any funds recovered by the sale of the property. In most states, the tax lien takes priority over any other form of lien held against the title to the property.

What this means is that you may request to take a position in the foreclosure proceedings. Since your lien takes priority, you will be paid in full before any other lien holder obtains funds from the sale. This occurs even when another party has instigated the foreclosure proceeding.

When holding a tax lien certificate you must also be aware of any actions that might affect your interest in the property beyond a court ordered foreclosure proceeding.

> Bankruptcy, divorce, an attempt to sell the property, and other instances where the ownership or interest in the property is being altered will effect your investment the same way it effects any lien holder in that property.

> You should always act to ensure you obtain a return on your investment any time the ownership or interest in the property is being altered.

Each State and specific Jurisdiction will use variations of the processes included in these chapters. It is wise to research the processes specific to your region before attending the sale. This manual has attempted to include information that will support your efforts regardless of the venue you choose for your new investment career. However, the wise investor will always keep in mind that regulations are consistently updated and that minor variations are created through State and Jurisdictional regulations. These variations will have an effect on your investment and investment strategy. This potential variance from the normal methods applied to tax sales makes researching your specific regulations as important to your future success as the completion of this coursework.

ADVANTAGES OF HOLDING A TAX LIEN

- **Priority**

  Tax liens are usually the highest priority line again the property.

  The priority of time is usurped by liens brought by a government entity for the non-payment of taxes so, if the property owner pays any item on record against the property for which you hold the lien, you will receive your money (investment + interest) before any other entity.

- **Higher investment yield**

  Interest rates on tax liens are often set at a higher rate than you will obtain through other investments.

  The purpose of the higher rate is twofold.

  > It penalizes the taxpayer for non-payment, encouraging timely payment of tax assessment billings received by the taxpayer.

  > It encourages investors to invest in tax liens, assisting in gaining the cash flow required by the government entity.

- **Higher security**

  The rate of taxation against the property is literally pennies on the dollar value of the property.

  What this means to the investor is that they are gaining a high security interest in the property.

  > Since tax liens often usurp the order of priority, the property owner will pay the tax lien first in the event of any sale, transfer or other liquidation attempt.

  > Since taxation rates are set at a low percentage of the overall value, your security in the investment is very high.

TAX LIEN CERTIFICATES PROCESS OVERVIEW

- The taxpayer fails to pay the delinquent taxes due on the property.

- A list is generated detailing all delinquent taxpayers and the property of each.

- The list is advertised in the newspaper to notify the public of the delinquency and potential sale of each property.

- A tax sale date is scheduled.

- At the sale, the tax liens totaling 1-2 years taxes + costs are auctioned in the order detailed on the tax sale list provided within the newspaper and on the day of the sale.

- The investor for each property offers a minimum or maximum bid. Some states allow for a minimum opening bid – the lowest possible interest rate that the investor will accept as part of the process.

- If the property does not receive any bids, it will not sell, however many states allow for a post sale offering opportunity. An excellent investment opportunity may exist following a sale and it may be prudent for you to review the post sale offerings following each sale. If unsold property is available, the bid for such a property may be placed via mail, over the counter or via the internet. The processes for the certificate issuance and post sale redemption requirements will remain the same, but the bidding process will not exist. When a property is purchased post sale using this method, your bid would be reviewed individually.

- At a regular certificate sale, the lowest interest bidder will be the winner. This bidder must pay the bid amount and any required fees to the taxing authority or company hired to conduct the sale. Payment will typically be made via cash or certified check.

- Upon receipt of the funds totaling the bid amount, the winning bidder will receive a certificate with the owners name, the legal amount of the lien, the interest rate for which the bid was awarded and the name of the investor. This lien must be recorded and become part of public record.

- Upon recordation, most states allow the tax lien to take priority overall other liens except municipal and IRS liens. This ability to usurp the typical order of priority promotes additional security for the investor.

- If the owner redeems the certificate during the post-sale redemption period, the investor receives the return of their investment funds and the interest awarded during the bidding process. This interest accumulation will vary by the specific sale that you attend. It may be assessed as simple daily interest or yearly interest assessed regardless of the date of payment. It is important to research the method that will apply to your investment because daily interest vs. yearly interest accumulations could dramatically affect the final value of your investment.

- If the owner does not redeem the certificate, additional tax assessments may accumulate against the property. If the property owner fails to pay the taxes assessed during periods AFTER your investment, additional tax liens may be created. It is important that you consider your position. You do not need to purchase future lien certificates but you should note that such certificates might exist. If you choose to apply for the deed to the property following the redemption period, you may be required to pay any secondary lien certificate investors the face value of their certificate plus interest and penalty accumulations in order to secure the property.

TAX LIEN POST REDEMPTION PROCESS

In most cases, the tax lien certificate will be recorded for you after you present payment for the successful bid. After recording, you simply wait to receive payment of the investment amount and the interest and penalties based on your winning bid. If the delinquent taxpayer does not make payment to you during the redemption period, additional tax liens may also be being created. You will want to consider whether to purchase these liens as part of your investment planning process. If you purchase all future liens that are created, you will hold a stronger position in the event that the certificate is not redeemed and you proceed to a foreclosure of the property to gain all rights to the deed. If you choose not to purchase future tax-lien certificates on the property, you should remember that these exist. Another investor may purchase these certificates and have their own investment plan. Your certificate will still maintain the priority of time, but the interest created through these other lines may effect your ultimate actions with regard to the use of the property. If you choose a foreclosure process as the result of your investment, you will be required to pay these liens and any penalty or interest awarded on these certificates as part of the process to clear your title.

It is also important that you consider that the condition of the title might change during the redemption period. If you have a certificate that is not being redeemed by the delinquent taxpayer, it is prudent to occasionally research the title from the date of the sale to determine if any additional matters have been recorded. If you proceed to a foreclosure process, these matters might become an issue that will effect your interest position.

If you choose to go through the process of foreclosing on the property through your tax lien certificate, you will bring a lawsuit. This lawsuit will be recorded in the Lis Pendens (Pending Lawsuit) index but you must also send a notice to all interest lien holders of your intent to foreclose.

The notice to all other lien holders or interested parties will typically take the form of a letter sent via certified mail or delivered personally. This letter will stipulate the date that the foreclosure proceeding will take place and offer the opportunity of any lien holders to appear and present any objections to the foreclosure or to reassert their interest. If a lien holder presents a valid interest or amount owed at the foreclosure proceeding, you will be responsible for making these payments in order to gain full rights to the property. Other tax-lien certificate holders may be one of the interested parties who come forth during the process.

You will file the complaint at the County Courts and request the date of the foreclosure proceeding. This complaint will detail your interest in the property, the default of payment required under your interest and request an order setting the time, place and amount of funds that must be paid in order to halt the foreclosure proceeding.

If no payment is made by the delinquent property owner, any interested parties will present themselves to the court and file notice of their interest in the property. If no lien holders present themselves, the court will issue a Final Judgment foreclosing the property in your favor and a Final Judgment will be recorded in the Clerk of Courts office. This then becomes a part of the public records system and finalizes your interest in the property as if it was a deed. The delinquent owner of the property will no longer hold an interest and no other parties may come forth and present liens after the date of the final judgment. It is important to note, the rights of any individual who you did not properly notify of the foreclosure proceeding will NOT be abolished. It is vital that you confirm the status of the title and ensure that all possible interested parties receive notice of the foreclosure proceeding.

You might consider using a real estate attorney to assist you with the foreclosure process. This will help you to gain a comprehensive understanding of the process and ensure that no steps or important matters are missed during your first few foreclosures.

If the property is occupied when you receive your final judgment of foreclosure, you will need to eject the occupants through the courts. To do so, you must request a Writ of Possession from the court at the time the Final Judgment be handed down. Upon receipt of the Writ of Possession request, the courts will notify the occupants that they must vacate the property. This process takes and average of 30 days but the actual period may vary depending upon the situation or jurisdiction. Upon expiration of the time provided under the notification to vacate you will proceed to the County Sheriff's offices and request a finalized eviction. The County Sheriff will schedule the eviction, serve the notices of final eviction and assist in removing any holdover occupants form the property. Upon completion of this process by the County Sheriff, you have access and all rights to the property and can begin implementing the steps dictated by your investment strategy.

WRAPPING UP - PRE AND POST SALE CHECKLIST

- Review the updated list and confirm your bidding list.

- Research all possible investments at the courthouse or hire an abstractor to conduct public records research for you.

- Drive by the property you are considering to determine the exact location, possible issues that may exist and occupancy status.

- Calculate the maximum bid that you are willing to place on each property. You might consider creating a relationship with a local real estate agent to assist you in gaining a better understanding of the potential values of the property you are considering before you determine how much you are willing to invest.

- Calculate expenses that you may incur to clear the title to the property.

- Detail a list of potential expenses you may incur to repair the property. This detail list will be modified based upon the interior of the property and you should remember that restoration expenses would play a factor if you gain the deed to the property.

- Ensure you have the cash on hand to meet your possible bid obligations. Most sales require that payment be made by cash or certified check within hours or days of the sale.

- Ensure that you have the required identification documents that will enable you to register and place bids at the sale. Many states require that you sign an affidavit stating that you are current on all property taxes for property you already hold and further require that you provide valid, photograph identification proving who you are prior to being authorized to bid at the sale.

- Arrive early on the day of the sale. At this time, you should review the property listing again. Many sales will allow for redemption by the property owner right up until the beginning of the sale.

- Review all notices provided by the taxing authority or company conducting the sale. These notices will finalize all of the applicable details of the sale and will highlight all disclaimers. If you have properly conducted your research before the sale, these notices should not contain any surprises.

- Be prepared for the structure of the sale.

  At most sales, an authorized individual will begin the process by reading all applicable notices.

They will then move through the list by reading the tax identification number of the property, the property address, block or lot ID.

Then they will state the minimum bid.

It is important that you understand the identifying methodology that will be used at any sale you attend. It may be prudent to attend a sale and watch the process prior to attending a sale for bidding. If you do not understand the identification methods used, you may accidentally bid on the wrong property or miss the opportunity to bid on a property of interest to you.

- When attending a lien sale, the bidding will typically begin at the highest rate allowed by law and bidders will bid downward to the lowest possible interest rate they will accept.

- When attending a deed sale, the bidding will typically begin at the lowest amount the taxing authority will accept and move upward in a standard auction style until only one-bidder remains.

- An individual will be responsible for noting the accepted bid for each property and the number of the winning bidder.

- Following the sale, the individual responsible for conducting the sale will provide a reminder of the acceptable methods of payment and provide you with instructions as to when and where you must make payment for your winning bids.

- You will follow the instructions and make payment for the items you won during the bidding process. Most commonly, you will proceed to the office of the Tax Collector to make payment.

- Upon receipt of the required payment, the individual authorized to issue such documents will issue you a receipt. This receipt will become a finalized tax lien certificate or a deed. These are usually mailed to the winning bidder within a set period after the sale. The period can range from 3 days to 90 days depending on the specific jurisdiction in which the sale is being conducted.

- If the taxing authority has not completed the recording actions for you, you should take your tax lien certificate or tax deed in the clerk of courts office. This notifies the public of your interest in the property through public notice within the public records system.

- If you have purchased a tax lien, you will await payment during the redemption period.

  If you do not receive a redemption payment, you should determine what your future goals with the property would be.

DO NOT allow the certificate to expire.

If another investor has purchased a tax certificate on the property, you may want to contact him or her to determine if he or she is interested in purchasing your certificate.

If tax certificates are created after the one you have purchased, you will want to decide if you wish to purchase those as well or if you are willing to allow another investor to hold a certificate in the same property.

If you choose to petition the courts for a lien foreclosure to gain access to the deed to the property, you will wish to conduct another search of public records to ensure that you have a full understanding of the obligations you may be taking on when you gain the deed.

- If you have purchased a tax deed at a free and clear sale, you are able to gain immediate access to the property upon confirmation of transfer from the taxing authority.

Following confirmation by the taxing authority, you should contact a reliable real estate attorney and instigate a quiet title suit.

This quiet title suit will clear the title and enable you to sell the property with good title in the future.

While awaiting the completion of the quiet title suit, you may begin restoration to the property, rent the property or take possession of the property in another manner.

CHAPTER

15

State-By-State Overview

The following list is generated from information provided by State and Regional taxing authorities. The author and the publisher make no warranty as to the accuracy of the information provided. The chart is included for the convenience of the reader and it is recommended that the reader confirm the information included before making any investment decisions. Every effort has been made to provide the most accurate and up-to-date information possible.

State	Deed Sale	Redemption Period	Certificate Sale	Average Return	Average Lien Redemption Period	Notes
Alabama	Yes	No	Yes	6%-12%	3 years	Bid Method – High Bid
Alaska	Yes	Yes	No	N/A	N/A	Bid Method – High Bid/ Sealed Bid
Arizona	No	N/A	Yes	16%	Varied - Typical 3 years	Bid Method – Bid Down Rate
Arkansas	Yes	Yes	No	N/A	N/A	Unsold deeds may be purchased after the sale Bid Method – High Bid / Mail In Bid

Figure 15:1 – Sample State Sale Guide – Page 1

State	Deed Sale	Redemption Period	Certificate Sale	Average Return	Average Lien Redemption Period	Notes
California	Yes	No	Yes	18%	Varied	Bid Method - High Bid
Colorado	No	N/A	Yes	Prime + 9%	Varied Typical 3 Years	Bid Method – High Bid
Connecticut	Yes	Yes – 1 year	No	N/A		If deed redeemed 18% return Bid Method – High Bid
Delaware	Yes	Yes – 1 year	No	N/A		If deed redeemed 15% return Bid Method – High Bid
Florida	Yes	None	Yes	18%	Varied – Typical 2 years	Bid Method Liens – Bid down rate Bid Method Deed – High Bid
Georgia	Yes	Yes – 1 year	Yes	20%	Varied	Bid Method – High Bid
Hawaii	Yes	Yes – 1 year	No	N/A	N/A	If deed redeemed – 12% return Bid Method – High Bid
Idaho	Yes	No	No	N/A	N/A	Bid Method – High Bid
Illinois	Yes	Yes	Yes	18%	2 year	Bid Method Lien – Bid Down Rate Bid Method Deed – High Bid

Figure 15:2 – Sample State Sale Guide – Page 2

State	Deed Sale	Redemption Period	Certificate Sale	Average Return	Average Lien Redemption Period	Notes
Indiana	Yes	Yes	Yes	25%	1 year	Bid Method – High Bid
Iowa	No	N/A	Yes	20%-24%	1-3 years	Bid Method – Bid Down
Kansas	Yes	No	No	N/A	N/A	Bid Method – High Bid
Kentucky	Yes	Yes	Yes	12%	Varied 3 years on liens	Bid Method - Varies
Louisiana	No	N/A	Yes	17%	Varied	Rate declines with longer redemption terms
Maine	Yes	Yes	No	N/A	N/A	
Maryland	Yes	Yes	Yes	24%	6 months – 1 year	
Massachusetts	Yes	Yes	Yes	16%	6 months	
Michigan	Yes	No	Yes	1st year interest 15% 2nd year interest 50%	1-3 years	
Minnesota	Yes	Yes	Yes	12%	3-5 years	

Figure 15:3 – Sample State Sale Guide – Page 3

State	Deed Sale	Redemption Period	Certificate Sale	Average Return	Average Lien Redemption Period	Notes
Mississippi	Yes	Yes	Yes	17%	2 years	Deed sale minimum bid is 50% of property value.
Missouri	No	N/A	Yes	10%	Varied	
Montana	Yes	Yes	Yes	Varied	3 years	
Nebraska	Yes	Yes	Yes	14%	Varied	
Nevada	Yes	Yes	Yes	12%	Varied	Raw land redemption and return vary.
New Hampshire	Yes	No	Yes	18%	2 years	
New Jersey	No	N/A	Yes	18%	2 years	
New Mexico	Yes	Yes	No	N/A	N/A	
New York	Yes	Yes	Yes	14%	Varied	
North Carolina	Yes	No	No	N/A	N/A	
North Dakota	Yes	No	No	N/A	N/A	None
Ohio	Yes	Yes	Yes	18%	Varied	Sale type contingent on population
Oklahoma	Yes	Yes	Yes	8%	2 years	

Figure 15:4 – Sample State Sale Guide – Page 4

State	Deed Sale	Redemption Period	Certificate Sale	Average Return	Average Lien Redemption Period	Notes
Oregon	Yes	Yes	No	N/A	N/A	
Pennsylvania	Yes	No	No	N/A	N/A	
Rhode Island	Yes	Yes	Yes	16%	1 year	Lien Certificate becomes Deed 1 yr
South Carolina	No	N/A	Yes	7%-8%	12-18 months	
Tennessee	Yes	Yes	No	Varied	1 year	If property redeemed 10% return is obtained
Texas	Yes	Yes	No	N/A	6 months – 2 years	If property redeemed, 25% return is obtained.
Utah	Yes	No	Yes	Varied	4 years	
Vermont	No	N/A	Yes	12%	1 year	
Virginia	Yes	No	No	N/A	N/A	
Washington	Yes	No	No	N/A	N/A	
West Virginia	Yes	Yes	Yes	12%	18 months	
Wisconsin	No	N/A	Yes	15%-18%	2 years	
Wyoming	No	N/A	Yes	18%	4 years	

Figure 15:3 – Sample State Sale Guide – Page 3
State information is provided by the applicable state agencies. The applicable data is for informational purposes only. All information is believed to be correct as of the time of printing; however, the reader should verify all data with the applicable county or state agency prior to generating an investment plan

APPENDIX B
GLOSSARY OF TERMS

Abstract of Title: the chronological history of the most relevant parts of every recorded instrument regarding a title

Abstractor : individual who specializes in research relevant to the chain of title

Abut: touch

Accretion: the build-up of soil caused by the action of water or wind

Accrue: to increase or accumulate. Mortgage interest is said to accrue daily

Acknowledgement: a declaration made before a notary or other official certifying that the signing of a document is of a voluntary act undertaken of ones own free will

Actual Notice: personal knowledge of an interest or instrument

Addendum: an attachment to a purchase agreement or to escrow instructions that alters or negotiates the transaction specifics

Ad Valorem: a Latin term that means 'according to value' Taxes are sometimes assessed on an ad valorem basis

Adverse Possession: obtaining title from another by the open, hostile, continuous use of property for a specific period set forth by statute

Affidavit: a statement sworn under oath or before a notary

Affirmation: a formal declaration regarding the truthfulness of a statement

Affirmative Easement: a type of easement that allows the easement holder the right to use the land of another landowner

Agency Disclosure: a disclosure made by real estate agents stating whom they represent in a specific transaction

Agreement of Sale: the real estate purchase contract

Air Rights: the rights to the use of the airspace located above a piece of property

Alienation Clause: a clause that calls an entire loan balance due and payable. This is also termed an acceleration clause or due on sale clause

Allodial System: a system of land ownership where the ownership is held by individuals rather than the government The US follows this system of ownership

Alluvion: the gradual addition of soil to a property by the action of water

Amendment: A change made to correct an error or to alter an agreement.

Amortization: The method by which a loan is paid down with each subsequent payment

Annual Percentage Rate: the yearly rate of interest on a loan

Antenuptial Agreement: an agreement executed between a man and a woman prior to marriage to resolve and settle future issues

Appropriation Process: The enactment of a taxing authority's budget and money sources into legally required payment.

Appurtenance: rights, benefits and attachments that transfer with real property

Appurtenant Easement: an easement that transfers with the land

Arrears: term used when describing a past due payment

ARM: adjustable rate mortgage

Assessed Value: the value placed on a property by the county assessor

Assessor's Map: The map that shows the assessor's parcel number for all land parcels within a specific taxing area

Assignment: the transfer, in writing, of one's interest in something

Assumption: the taking over of another person's financial obligation

Balloon Payment: the final payment that pays a note in full

Bankruptcy: a legal procedure that eliminates unsecured debt or relinquishes property to eliminate secured debt

Bargain and Sale Deed: a deed that uses the term bargain and sale and contains no warranties other than implied interest on the part of the seller

Base Line: Latitude line that acts as a reference in the rectangular survey system

Binder: insurance coverage given by an agent prior to the issuance of the full insurance policy

Bundle of Rights: all rights of ownership of real property. Synonym for estate

Certificate of Title: evidence of title issued by a registrar

Cession Deed: deed that conveys all rights of an individual in real property to a county or municipality

Chain of Title : the history, in chronological order, of a property from the original government grant to the present owner

Close of Escrow: the date when the documents are recorded and title passes from the seller to the buyer

Closing Costs: the costs that are payable to close escrow not including the purchase price of a property

Cloud on Title: a claim, document, defect or discrepancy that casts doubt on the marketability of a title

Collateral: real or personal property pledged as security for a loan

Commitment of Title: the guarantee from a title company that they will provide title insurance Also termed a preliminary title report

Competent: legally qualified to conduct transactions

Concurrent Escrow: a procedure where the one closing is dependent on the completion of another closing Also termed a double escrow

Condemnation: the legal action to take a property for public use by eminent domain

Consideration: the amount of money or services given in exchange for the transfer of a property

Constructive Notice: the notice given by occupancy or recording of an interest in real property

Contingency: a condition that must be met or event that must happen before a contract will be considered binding

Convey: the transfer of title from one person to another

Covenant: a written agreement as to the use of a property

Declaration of Restriction: declaration of the restrictions contained in a deed of conveyance

Deed: a document that conveys interest and title to real property

Deed in Lieu of Foreclosure: a deed from a property owner to a lien holder made to avoid full foreclosure proceedings.

Deemer Period: the method that the state regulates the rate of filing by the title company

Deficiency Judgment: a judgment obtained when the foreclosure sale does not satisfy a debt in full

Descent: the hereditary succession by law when a property owner dies without a valid will

Determinable Fee Estate: an estate that would end on the occurrence of a specific event

Dominant Estate: an estate for which an easement is granted

Disbursement : the release of funds held in an escrow account

Earnest Money: a deposit by a buyer to a seller to bind an agreement

Easement: the right of a person to use the land of another

Easement by Necessity: an easement granted out of a valid need for the easement

Easement by Prescription: an easement created by the open, continuous, hostile and notorious use of the property of another for a specified period of time

Easement in Gross: a personal easement to use the land of another in which no dominant estate exists

Emblements: cultivated crops that are considered personal property

Eminent Domain: the government's right to take private property for public use with just compensation paid to the property owner for the loss

Encroachment: the unauthorized intrusion on, over or under the land of another

Encumbrance : any item that affects the title to real property such as liens, easements or deed restrictions

Endorsement: an addition that either expands or limits the standard coverage provided under a title insurance policy

Escrow: the act of depositing papers and or money with an impartial third party until a transaction is complete

Escrow Instructions: a series of instructions from a buyer, seller, lender or other interested party as to the acts that must be completed and conditions that must be met prior to the transfer of a property

Equitable Title: title obtained during the period between the creation of an agreement or contract and the finalization of a transaction

Escheat: the reversion of a property to the state when a person dies without a valid will and no heirs as identified by statute

Exception in Deed: exclusion in a deed that deeds only one portion of a property

Execute to validate a document

Fee Simple Estate: the highest level of ownership possible the fee simple ownership includes the full bundle of rights

Fee Simple Determinable: a grant that ends if a property is not longer used for a designated purpose

Fee Tail Estate: an estate that limits conveyance to the heirs and decedents of the owner

Fixture: an item of personal property that is permanently attached to real property in a manner that causes it to become real property

Foreclosure: a legal process that deprives an owner of his or her rights to a property

Funding: the release of loan money from a lender to the escrow company

General Warranty Deed: a deed where the grantor warrants title against the claims of all others

Gift Deed: a deed that transfers real property for love and affection rather than valuable consideration

Good Consideration: love and affection are considered good consideration

Grant: the act of conveying title to a property

Grantee: the person who receives a deed, grant or other item

Granting Clause: a deed provision showing that title is passing

Grantor: the person giving or conveying the deed, grant or other item

Grantor/Grantee Index: an index system for researching chain of title that lists grantor/grantee names

Guardianship : the administration of the property of a minor or incompetent person

Habendum: a to have and to hold clause indicating the extent of the ownership being transferred

Impound: to accumulate borrower funds to meet the periodic payments due under tax billings or insurance billings

Improvement: an addition to land that is considered real property

Indemnity: a guarantee against loss

Incompetent: a person who is deemed incapable of making a legal decision or entering a legal contract due to age or mental capacity

Informal Reference: a description of property that uses items such as number, street or addresses This is not a legal description of property

Instrument: a written legal document such as a sales agreement, contract or promissory note

Inverse Condemnation: an action instituted by a property owner forcing the government to take property where the property use is restricted by an action taken by the government or other public entity

Involuntary Lien: a lien imposed without the consent of a property owner

Joint Tenancy: an undivided interest that contains all unities except the unity of person

Judgment: the order by a court as to money owed or other definitive decisions

Judgment in Personam: a judgment against a person When recorded the judgment becomes a specific lien against a particular property of the person involved in the action

Judgment in Rem: a judgment against specific property When recorded the judgment becomes a specific lien against the property involved in the action

Judicial Foreclosure: a foreclosure that requires court proceedings for finalization

Jurat: the statement or certificate of the individual witnessing signatures to specific instruments

Legal Access: the legal right to use a specified access point

Legal Description: a description of real property that can be considered legally binding

Lender Instructions: the instructions received from a lender stating the requirements that must be met before a transaction can be closed

Lien: a monetary encumbrance secured by real property

Life Estate: an estate that exists for the lifetime of a specific person

Lis Pendens: pending lawsuit

Littoral rights: the rights of a property owner to the use of a lake, pond or ocean water that borders his or her property in a reasonable manner

Marketable Title: a title that is clear of liens, encumbrances and other defects

Mechanic's Lien: a specific lien against real property placed by a contractor for work performed to the property or property improvements when the charges are not paid as agreed by the property owner

Meridians: north-south lines used by government surveyors for measuring and describing real property

Metes and Bounds: a method of legal description by measurement and boundary of real property

Monument: a fixed marker used in surveys within the metes and bounds method

Mutual Consent: approval of both parties regarding the terms of a contract

Negotiable: able to be assigned or transferred

Notary Public: the person enabled by the property authorities to witness signatures, oaths or other matters

Offset Statement: the statement by an owner or lien holder detailing the liens against a piece of property

Option: a right given by the owner of property to another to buy a property at an agreed upon price and within an agreed upon time

Personal Property: property that is not classified as real property

Physical Access: access is the actual ability to use an access point

Police Power: the power of the state to enforce laws to promote the health and safety of the general public through the taking of a privately held piece of land

Post-nuptial Agreement: an agreement executed between a husband and wife following marriage to determine and settle specific issues

Preliminary Title Report: a report indicating the present condition of the title based on items discovered during a record search

Prescription: an easement obtained by the open, hostile, continuous and notorious use of another's property for a regulated period of time

Prior Appropriation: a theory used in some states that allows the first user to divert water to maintain that sole interest in the water even though the use may not be equitable to other landowners

Priority: taking place in order or precedence over. In a real estate transaction, priority is typically established by the date of the recording of an instrument or specific wording within an instrument. Priority may be usurped by the government right of taxation

Proration: the method employed to divide taxes, interest and other sums between a buyer and a seller based upon a certain date

Quiet Enjoyment: the right of an owner to use their property without interference

Quiet Title: a court action to obtain a determination regarding ownership right

Quitclaim Deed: a deed conveying whatever interest a grantor holds in real property. This type of deed makes no claim to actual ownership

Real Property: land and all that goes with the land

Recordation: the act of recording valid documents with the office of record to serve notice to all regarding the instruments recorded

Redemption: the act of reclaiming the title to property from someone who has taken legal interest in it

Redemption Period: the time in which an individual may redeem the interest in his or her property

Release: the relinquishment or giving up of a specific right or claim of interest

Remainder Interest: an interest obtained by a third party after the expiration of a life estate

Reservation: a specific right withheld by the grantor when conveying property

Restrictive Covenant: a restriction where the owner is limited as to the use of his or her property

Reversionary Interest: an interest to a property by the original grantor following the occurrence of a specific event

Right of Way: the right to pass over the land of another

Riparian Rights: rights of a landowner to use flowing water located on, under or adjacent to his or her property in a reasonable manner

Security: the property pledged to secure the repayment of a loan

Servient Estate: an estate that bears the burden of an easement

Settlement: the time at which a property transfer is finalized

Sheriff's Deed: a deed given by a sheriff when a property is sold for the execution of a judgment or at foreclosure sale

Special Warranty Deed: a deed where the seller warrants the title only against defects occurring during his or her ownership

Specific Lien: a lien against a particular piece of property

Statute of Limitations: the time limit within which legal proceedings may be implemented and action brought

Subject To: to take title without paying off one or more existing liens or notes

Sub-surface Rights: the right to the space and natural resources contained below the surface of a particular parcel of land

Surface Rights: the right to use the surface of a parcel of land Commonly known as the rights to the land and the improvements of the land

Survey: a verification of property lines or the creation of a legal description created by a surveyor

Survivorship: the right of a joint tenant to obtain the interest of another tenant upon the death of the other party or other event that negates the interest of the other party

Tax Deed: a deed obtained as a result of a tax sale

Tenancy: method of holding ownership or interest in a property

Tenancy by the Entirety: a form of joint tenancy held by husband and wives and containing all of the forms of unity

Tenancy in Common: a form of joint tenancy by two or more individuals or entities where each obtains an undivided interest in real property

Title: ownership Title is passed by deed

Title Insurance: the insurance policy that agrees to indemnify the insured against defects in the title

Vendee: buyer

Vendor: seller

Vest: to convey or confer

Vesting: the manner in which title to real property is held Method of interest in real property

Void: having no legal effect

Voidable: capable of being voided or valid only until voided

Voluntary Lien: a lien created by the action of the property owner in consideration of money borrowed

Waiver: the release of a right

PROPERTY DATA FORM

Property Address: _____

Map Number: _____ Tax Identification Number: _____

Assessed Value: _____ Zoning: _____

Legal Description

Site Drawing / Dimensions

Improvements: _____
_____
_____

Photograph 1

Photograph 2

Figure 12:1 – Sample Property Data Form – Page 1

Current Owner: _____

Current Co-Owner: _____

Lis Pendens Index	Date	Amounts	Status

Mortgage	Date	Amounts	Status

Judgments / Liens	Date	Amounts	Status

Previous Sales/Comparables	Date	Amounts	Notes

Figure 12:2 – Sample Property Data Form – Page 2

UPCOMING SALE DATA COLLECTION – TAX ASSESSOR

COUNTY: _____   TELEPHONE NUMBER: _____

When is the next scheduled tax sale auction?		
How many sales do you offer per year?		
What are the dates of the sales?		
What types of sales are they?		
Where may I obtain a list of the property to be sold?		
What are the registration pre-requites?		
What types of payment do you accept?		
What is the bidding process for the sale?		
May I bid by proxy?	Yes	No
What is the method for bidding by proxy?	Sealed	Phone/Internet
Do you have a web site that contains the list?	Yes	No
Address		
Do you have a web site that enables a preliminary records search?	Yes	No
Web Address		
What happens to liens/deeds that are not sold at the sale?		
Can unsold liens/deeds be purchased from the county after the sale?	Yes	No
What is the process for counter purchases of unsold liens/deeds/		
Are there liens/deeds available over the counter now?	Yes	No
How do I obtain a list of available liens/deeds for over the Counter purchase?		
Is there a post-sale redemption period?	Yes	No
How long is the post sale redemption?		
Will I incur additional costs beyond the bid amount when I win a property?	Yes	No
What are these costs?		

Figure 12:3 – Sample Sale Data Form

www.ingramcontent.com/pod-product-compliance
Lightning Source LLC
Chambersburg PA
CBHW080330270326
41927CB00014B/3164

* 9 7 8 1 9 3 3 0 3 9 6 3 3 *